POPULATION GROWTH IN ASSAM
1951-1991
WITH FOCUS ON MIGRATION

POPULATION GROWTH IN ASSAM 1951-1991

WITH FOCUS ON MIGRATION

By

Anil Saikia
Homeswar Goswami
Atul Goswami

AKANSHA PUBLISHING HOUSE
NEW DELHI-110 059 (INDIA)

thousand in 1911. Enumerated first in 1911 on the *char* lands of Goalpara, these migrants in the words of 1961 Census Superintendent, Pakyntein, were 'merely the advance guards or rather scouts of a huge army following closely on their heels'. In the subsequent two decades the migrants advanced towards the districts of Nowgong, Kamrup (the then Barpeta sub-division) and Darrang. By 1931 most of the waste lands of the Brahmaputra Valley was already occupied by the settlers. By 1941 they penetrated the then North Lakhimpur district. After Saadullah became the Premier of Assam for the second time in August 1942, it is alleged that he attempted a systematic settlement of East Bengal Muslim peasants in Assam under the pretext of raising the state's agricultural production (Grow More Food Campaign). In fact, this is believed to be a part of the design of some Muslim leaders to convert Assam into a Muslim dominated area. No wonder, when the demand for Partition was raised, it was visualized by the Muslim League leaders that Pakistan would comprise Muslim majority provinces in the West and Bang-E-Islam comprising Bengal and Assam in the East.

The third stream of migrants consisted of Bengali Hindu refugees mostly from the then Sylhet district to the adjoining areas of present Assam and Tripura as a result of Partition. Persons born in Pakistan and enumerated in Assam reached the enormous total of 800 thousand. Of course this huge number included a large number of refugees (262 thousand) born in Pakistan migrating to Assam during the Partition. (*Census of India, 1951, Assam, General Report*).

The setting up of the two Dominions of India and Pakistan did not prove deterrent to the Muslim settlers who continued to pour even after Partition. (*Census of India, 1961, Assam, General Report, ibid.*) But what was till then migration from one part of the same country to another, became in the eyes of law, immigration of Pakistani nationals into the north eastern region. Bengali Hindus, in particular, from the then East Pakistan continued to pour into Assam and Tripura because of recurring communal troubles there. In Assam the number of Bengali Hindu refugees went up from 2.62 lakh in 1951 to 6.0 lakh in 1961. This decade also witnessed a large inflow of migrants from other parts of India seeking economic opportunities in trading, construction work, and white collar jobs.

Another stream of migrants into the North East in general and Assam in particular, which went more or less unnoticed, consisted of Nepali graziers, who, from the beginning of the 20th century, started settling in the uncultivated and un-owned hill slopes. The number of Nepalis in Assam alone went up from 1.01 lakh in 1951 to 3.54 lakh in 1971.

In 1971 during the Bangladesh Liberation War a large number of persons from erstwhile East Pakistan fled to Assam and other units of the north east, some of whom might not have returned to the place of origin even after the formation of Bangladesh as a separate country.

It is obvious from the above that the various census reports provide a rough estimate of migrants coming to Assam in particular from 1951 to 1971. In 1981, census operation could not be undertaken in the state of Assam. The 1981 census reports of the other states of the north eastern region, however, indicate that migration from Bangladesh and Nepal continued unabated. In Assam the fear of illegal migrants (resulting from unchecked flow even during the post-1971 period) outnumbering the indigenous population led to a six year prolonged movement starting from 1979. This fear is still haunting the Assamese psyche.

There is a total absence of an estimate of post-1971 migrants to Assam in particular based on sound demographic tools to the north eastern region of India. This has led to wild guesses made by different interest groups to suit their convenience. It is in this context of putting a check to this unhealthy practice that an objective estimate of the post-1971 migrants in particular has become imperative.

Initially, objective of the study was to provide a scientific explanation of the phenomenal growth of population of the north eastern region of India, state-wise and district-wise during 1951-1991 in terms of the various components of population growth viz. fertility, mortality and migration, with special focus on migration.

Although the ambit of the original study proposal covered all the units of North-East India, considering the vastness of the area and resource constraints, both financial and manpower, it was decided later to conduct the study taking the state of Assam first and subsequently extending it to cover other units of the region, exploring meanwhile the possibility of mobilizing adequate funds from appropriate agencies for the purpose. Hence the book deals with the population growth in Assam during 1951-1991 with focus on migration.

The work is divided into six chapters. The first chapter spells out the methodology of the study, besides stating the objectives and database. It provides the rationale behind the decision of adopting the census survival method for estimating the volume of migration, despite the fact that other methods are also available and used by none.

The second chapter discusses the issues relating to smoothening of census age data. It is to be noted that we have tried to find out the magnitude of migration in each quinquennial age group for each of the four dreads covered by the study. But testing the census 5-year age population distribution data by United Nations Secretariat Index (UNSI), it was found that the age and sex ratio accuracy index was not satisfied by the Assam census age specific distribution of data. In order to make the age group wise distribution of population in conformity with the UNSI, the population distribution was smoothened by using the moving average method. In addition, the Grouped Age Ratio Adjusted Multiplier (GARAM), an innovation, was applied for further smoothening the census age group data.

The third chapter is devoted to the task of constructing life tables for Assam relating to the decades 1961-71, 1971-81 and 1981-91 and for the period 1971-91, (since age specific mortality rates of Assam for the decade 1951-61 are not available, the life table constructed by Kohli for the decade 1951-61 is used), as it is only the life table which provides us the age specific survival ratio so as to enable us to arrive at age specific population in a succeeding census from the age specific population distribution of the preceding census. The life tables are constructed taking the age specific mortality rates as estimated by the SRS. But the age specific mortality rates as furnished by the SRS are found to be highly fluctuating which have therefore been smoothened by fitting regression equations. The chapter also makes an estimate of sex specific, infant and child mortality rates. In the succeeding chapter the estimating procedure adopted for ascertaining decade wise births has been described. Sex specific births have also been worked out in the same chapter.

Survivors in the age group 0-4 and 5-9 in the census years 1961 and 1971 and age groups from 0-4 to 15-19 for the census year 1991 have been estimated in the fifth chapter.

The sixth chapter incorporates the findings of the study. It provides alternative estimates of migrants to Assam during the study period based on various methods. The first set of estimates is based on the census place of birth data. The reason for rejecting these estimates is also furnished.

Next, decade wise estimates of migrants are worked out by applying the vital statistics method. This is followed by estimates obtained by applying the survival ratio method. Although both the indirect methods yield almost similar estimates of migrants, the latter method is preferred as it is considered more scientific. According to the survival ratio method, net immigration to Assam during 1951-61, 1961-71 and 1971-91 stood at 1067846, 801880 and 976969 respectively totalling 2846695 for the study period as a whole.

Although an extremely difficult task, an attempt is also made in this chapter to split the estimated migrants into (i) inter-state and international and (ii) legal and illegal.

Finally, in order to ascertain the total effect of the migrants on the growth of Assam's population during the study period, we have calculated the offspring of the migrants by applying Assam's natural growth rate to the migrant population. Taking the offspring together with the migrants, Assam's population is found to have increased by 49,15,058 during 1951-1991. The chapter ends with citing the major limitations of the study.

The study team originally constituted included a large number of names, all of whom made some contribution to the contents of the book. But the hard work of drafting the manuscript fell almost fully on Dr. Anil Saikia, a promising demographer. He deserves credit for completing the work so aptly within the given time frame. Professor Homeswar Goswami, a renowned demographer teaching at Dibrugarh University, certified the demographic soundness of the work after going through the manuscript by taking out time from his busy schedule. Co-ordination and general supervision have been my role.

I take this opportunity of expressing my gratitude and sincere thanks to each of the members of the Team for providing the necessary intellectual input.

Sri M.P. Misra, proprietor, M/s Akansha Publishing House, New Delhi deserves special thanks for bringing out the book.

Atul Goswami

CONTENTS

The Team

A. Advisors :

Professor J. P. Medhi	Professor Emeritus, Department of Statistics, Gauhati University
Professor H.K. Borpujari	Retired Professor, Gauhati University
Professor Amalendu Guha	Retired Professor, Centre for Studies in Social Sciences, Calcutta
Professor B.K. Roy Burman	Retired Professor, Santiniketan, West Bengal
Shri N.C. Dutta, IAS	Ex-Director of Census Operation, Assam
Director	Omeo Kumar Das Institute of Social Change and Development

B. Consultants :

Professor Atul Sarma	Indian Statistical Institute, New Delhi
Prof. Biswanath Bhattacharya	Indian Statistical Institute, Calcutta
Professor D.C. Nath	Department of Statistics, Gauhati University
Shri Labananda Choudhury	Department of Statistics, Gauhati University
Shri Jogesh Bhuyan	Retired Deputy Director, Census Operation, Assam

C. Study Team :

Professor Atul Goswami	Omeo Kumar Das Institute of Social Change and Development
Prof. Homeswar Goswami	Department of Economics, Dibrugarh University
Dr. Anil Saikia	Department of Economics, Moran College, Moran
Dr. Indranee Dutta	Omeo Kumar Das Institute of Social Change and Development
Dr. Bhupen Sharma	Omeo Kumar Das Institute of Social Change and Development
Dr. Kalyan Das	Omeo Kumar Das Institute of Social Change and Development
Mr. Rustam Ali	Omeo Kumar Das Institute of Social Change and Development

1

INTRODUCTION

Although there is a general agreement that migrants, interstate as well as international, continue to constitute an important component of Assam's population even during 1951 to 1991, no firm estimates based on sound demographic tools are available. This has led to wild guesses of immigrants ranging from 2 lakh to 77 lakh at various points of time made by different interest groups to suit their convenience[1]. Such guess estimates are more plentiful for the period 1971-1991 as the 1981 census could not be conducted in Assam. Consequently widely divergent estimates of migrants are found for this period. It is therefore desirable to put at rest the speculation on the issue.

The study is based on the census definition of 'migration'. 'Till 1961, migration data were collected and presented with reference to the place of birth. . If a person was born at a place other than the place of enumeration, he was treated as a migrant in census returns. In censuses upto 1951, a question on birth place was asked. The data presented related to the number of migrants by sex. In 1961 census, an effort was made to widen the scope of enquiry and collected information on : (i) Birth-place statistics, (ii) Birth-place (rural and urban), (iii) Duration of residence if born elsewhere. But these statistics did not account for the more recent movement of a person. Thus a person who had migrated elsewhere for all practical purposes and happened to be at the place of birth during the period of enumeration, was treated as a non-migrant at the census.

In 1971 census migration data were collected for the first time on the basis of place of last residence in addition to the question of birth place. The question were – I, Birth-place, (a) place of birth, (b) rural/ urban, (c) district, (d) state/country, II. Last residence, (i) (a) place of last residence, (b) rural/urban, (c) district, (d) state/country, (ii) duration of residence at the village or town of enumeration.

In 1981 census, the scope of enquiry on migration was further widened by collecting information on 'reasons for migration from place of last residence.' The reasons for migration from place of last residence included in 1981 census were (a) Employment, (b) Education, (c) Family moved, (d) Marriage and (e) others. In 1991 census, two more reasons namely 'business' and 'natural calamities like drought, floods, etc.' were added.'[2]

'The migration tables of the 1991 census are mainly based on the questions on place of birth, place of last residence, duration of residence at the place of enumeration and reason for migration (Question 18-21) included in the individual slip. These tables generated on computer provide the distribution of population by place of birth, distribution of migrants by place of last residence duration of residence and reason for migration. The data on intra-districts intra-state and inter-state migration streams and in-migration from abroad are presented in these tables. Information on educational level and work participation of migrants are also available in the migration tables.

In the 1991 census 18 tables have been prepared on migration. Of these 15 tables are based on a 10 per cent sample in states with a population of 10 million and above and on full count basis in the remaining states and union territories. The remaining 3 tables dealing with migrants among main workers other than cultivators and agricultural labourers have been prepared on the basis of full count in all states and union territories.'[3]

Objective

The primary objective of this study is to provide a scientific explanation of the growth of population in Assam during 1951 to 1991 in terms of various components of population growth viz. fertility, mortality and migration, with focus on migration. The exercise is conducted decade-wise and age group-wise.

Data Base

The study is based on census population data[4] and SRS (Sample Registration System) estimates of fertility and mortality rates[5].

Methodology

As mentioned above, one of the aims of the present study is to make an objective estimate of the net volume of migration into Assam since 1951. There are two main methods for estimating migration (in or out) -

(1) Direct method
(2) Indirect method

Direct Method

The census birth place statistics provide the only direct method of estimating migration to a State. But the accuracy of the estimates is dependent on the respondents' answer relating to the 'place of birth' question, which has to be recorded by the enumerator as reported. If respondents willfully give wrong 'birth place' information, which is usually the practice of many of the illegal migrants, then the net volume of migration based on such information is bound to be incorrect. This phenomenon is predominantly found in Indian censuses. This is corroborated by Pakyntein's statement which is reproduced below. (Pakyntein was the Superintendent of Census operations, Assam, 1961). "Birth place statistics appeared to be completely unreliable in 1961. Our experience during enumeration as well as tabulation is that people did not correctly give their place of birth and so the interpretation of data is very limited. True migration is often artificially deflated and remigration to the place of birth is masked. It appears that the people who mostly concealed their birth- place are those coming from East Pakistan. In 1951, people who returned their birth-place as Pakistan number 831,872 but in 1961 the number of such people is only 774,869 ....The slips in my tabulation office indicate that the Hindus generally gave their birth-place correctly but among the Muslims almost everyone gave his birth-place as Assam .These incorrect statements have reached such serious proportion that it is no longer possible for me to make any reliable conclusion from migration data."[6] In the same vein, Dey (the Assistant Director of Census Operation, Technical Assam 1971) expresses his doubts about the number of immigrants into Assam as recorded in 1971 census. He states, 'this figure is also not reliable and cannot be used to make any valid estimate of growth of either immigrants themselves or the total population of the State excluding immigrants'[7]

Taking into account the inaccuracies of census place of birth statistics, one is left with no alternative but to use indirect methods for arriving at estimates of migration, consistent with fertility and mortality rates.

Indirect Methods

The indirect methods of estimating the volume of in and out migration consist of the following

(1) Residual Method or Vital Statistics Method

The simplest equation to estimate net migration by this method is expressed as -

$$M = (P_1 - P_0) - (B - D) \;\ldots\ldots\ldots\ldots (1)$$

or

$$P_1 = P_0 + (B - D) \pm M$$

Where **M** stands for net migration (in or out) between two consecutive censuses. P_1 and P_0 stand respectively for population of succeeding and preceding censuses, **B** stands for total number of births and **D** for the total number of deaths between these two consecutive censuses. Data relating to these are readily available in various census reports and other reports on vital statistics.

According to the above formula, migration in the second census is equal to the difference of the differences between (a) the two consecutive census populations and (b) total births and deaths during the intercensal period.

Alternatively, population of second census is equal to the sum of the first census population and the difference of births and deaths and migration, if any, between the two censuses.

(2) Survival Rate Method

The survival rate method is the commonly used variant in statistically underdeveloped countries because it does not require accurate vital statistics. It is also frequently used in statistically developed countries as well, partly because it yields estimates of net migration by age and sex without nearly as much labour as is involved in the use of death by age.[8] There are two survival rate methods to estimate migration. These are as follows -

(a) Forward Survival Rate Method

$$M_1 = P_1^a - S\,P_{0-t}^a \quad \ldots\ldots\ldots\ldots\ldots (2)$$

(b) Reverse Survival Rate Method

$$M_2 = P_1^a/s - P_{0-t}^a \quad \ldots\ldots\ldots\ldots\ldots (3)$$

The average of estimates M_1 and M_2 gives M_3

$$M_3 = (M_1 + M_2)/2 \quad \ldots\ldots\ldots\ldots\ldots (4)$$

Where S is the survival rate, $\mathbf{P_1^a}$ and $\mathbf{P_{0}^{a}{}_{-t}}$ are populations of age group 'a' and 'a-t' of two consecutive censuses. The population of age groups 'a-t' and 'a' are known as the 'cohorts" and 'survivors' respectively. A cohort of a particular age or age group becomes the survivor in the next census in the age or age group, advanced by 10 years. If survival ratios of the ages or age groups are available, then the number of survivors in the ages or age groups advanced by 10 years (i.e. in the next census) can be easily estimated. A difference between the census populations in the ages or age groups (in the next census) and the survivors of the corresponding age or age groups can then be assumed as net migration (in or out). For instance, the cohorts of 0-4 age group in 1951 became the survivors of 10-14 age group in 1961 census. If the cohort of 0-4 age group in 1951 was 1000, survival rate 0.986 and the census population of 1961 in the 10-14 age group 999, then the net migration in the age group 10-14 in 1961 would be as follows -

(a) Forward Survival Rate Method

$$\mathbf{M_1 = 999 - .986 \times 1000 = 13}$$

(b) Reverse Survival Rate Method

$$\mathbf{M_2 = 999/.986 - 1000 = 13.18}$$

(c) Average estimate

$$\mathbf{M_3 = (13 + 13.18) / 2 = 13.09 \text{ or } 13}$$

Estimating Migration by Survival Rate Method

The main requirements to estimate age and sex specific migration by reverse and forward survival rate methods are –

1. Smoothened quinquennial age group population by sex of the census years 1951, 1961, 1971,1981 and 1991. (estimates of age specific population for 1981 census were not available);

2. Life tables by sex of the decades 1951-61, 1961-71, 1971-81, 1981-91 and period 1971-91 to estimate age and sex specific survival ratios;

3. 5-year age and sex specific mortality rates of the decades 1951-61 to 1981-91 in order to construct life tables;

4. Birth rates of the decades 1951-61 to 1981-91 in order to estimate survivors in the age groups 0-4 and 5-9, as the survival ratios give projected population from age group 10-14 onward in general; and

5. Sex specific infant mortality rates for the decades 1951-61 to 1981-91.

Data available

1. Age and sex specific quinquennial age group population for the census year 1951, 1961, 1971 and 1991;

2. Life table for the decade 1951-1961 as constructed by Kohli[9];

3. SRS age and sex specific mortality rates by quinquennial age groups for constructing Life table for the decades 1961-71,1971-81,1981-91 and period 1971-91;

4. The census birth rates for the decades 1957-61 and 1961-71 and SRS birth rates since 1968.

For establishing the accuracy, the age specific census data are to be tested and smoothened. These are done in the second chapter. The third chapter is devoted to the construction of life tables for 1961-71, 1971-81, 1981-91 and 1971-91, while the fourth chapter estimates the number of births. The fifth chapter gives the number of survivors in the age group 0-4 and 5-9. The concluding chapter (the sixth chapter) provides the estimates of migration by applying different methods.

Noteworthy that there is yet another method for estimating migration, namely, "National Growth Rate Method". Although it is a commonly used method for estimating the rate of internal migration, it requires the fulfilment of a condition that the 'rates of natural increase and of net immigration from abroad are the same for all parts of the country'[10]. Hence, no estimate by using this method is done in this study.

References

1. For details see M. Hussain, *The Assam Movement*, Monak Publication Pvt. Ltd., Delhi, 1993, pp. 133-135

2. *Census of India, Assam* : 1991, Series – 4, Migration Tables, Vol. 1, p. 1

3. *ibid,* p.V

4. *Census of India, Assam* : 1951, 1961, 1971, and 1991

5. SRS Analytical Series, No. 2, 1972, *Measures of Fertility and Mortality in India,* 1968-69, Registrar General India, 1972, and *Compendium of India's Fertility and Mortality Indicators*, 1971-97, Registrar General India, 1999

6. Quoted in *Census of India, 1971, Assam*, General Report, Series – 3, Part I-A, p. 10

7. K.S. Dey, *Census of India 1971, Assam, ibid,* p. 10

8. H.S. Shyrock, *et. al, Methods and Materials of Demography*, Academic Press, New York, 1976, p. 379

9. K.L. Kohli, *Mortality in India*, Sterling Publishers Pvt. Ltd., New Delhi, 1977, pp. 228 - 231

10. *ibid*, p. 378

2

SMOOTHENING OF CENSUS AGE DATA

Inaccuracy in the census age data is an established fact and common to the most of the countries of the world. The errors in the age returns arise from the reasons like (i) digit preference, specially with the digits ending in 5 and 0 and generally with the digits ending in 2,4,6 and 8, (ii) deliberately making understatement of age in the earlier phase of life and overstatement of age in the latter phase, (iii) ignorance of true age because of the absence of the practice of compulsory birth registration etc. These factors cause erroneous age distribution even in the advanced countries where most of the people are literate and conscious of their age. Therefore, the census age data require smoothening to make them useful for demographic analysis including estimating migration. [1]

For the sake of convenience, we propose to find out the magnitude of migration in each quinquennial age group. Hence, the study requires only 5-year age group smoothened population data. Therefore, instead of testing single year age data, (i.e. test of digit preference with the digit ending in 5 and 0, index of concentration in each digit), only 5-year age group data are considered for testing. It is observed that 5-year group age data are comparatively less distorted. Because 'where the data are grouped into 5-year age groups or broader groups, both the gross and net misreporting errors are smaller, than the corresponding errors for single ages since misreporting of age within the boarder intervals has no effects. On the other hand, the amount of net under-enumeration will tend to accumulate and grow as the age interval widen, since omissions will tend to exceed erroneous inclusions at each age. For the total population, the amount of net under-enumeration and amount of net census undercount are the same since net age misreporting balance out to zero over all ages'.[2] Although, in the grouped age data the net misreporting tends to balance out to zero over the ages, nevertheless, the census 5-year group age data are also found to suffer from age distortion. Therefore 5-year age group data are further tested by United Nations Secretariat Indices (UNSI) i.e. age and sex ratio accuracy index for the census years 1951, 1961, 1971 and 1991. The method of working out UNSI is as follows -

Age Ratio

Age ratio is defined as a percentage between the population of a given age group (P_1) and mean population of the age groups, P_0, P_1 and P_2.

$$\text{Age ratio} = \frac{P_1}{(P_0 + P_1 + P_2)/3} \times 100$$

Sex Ratio

Sex ratio for this method is defined as number of males per 100 females.

Joint Score or United Nations Secretariat Index or United Nations Age Sex Accuracy Index

U.N. age sex accuracy index is a combined sum of (a) the mean deviation of the age ratios for males from 100 (b) the mean deviation of the age ratios for females from 100 and (c) three times the mean of the succeeding and preceding age group difference of the sex ratios. (It is to be noted that while calculating mean deviation and difference signs are ignored).

The steps involved in the methods are as follows -

1. Mean of age ratios :

(a) Age ratios are to be calculated separately for male and female;

(b) Age ratios are to be subtracted from 100 and summed up by ignoring the signs; and

(c) Sums of the deviations of both sexes are to be divided by total number of age ratios for obtaining the mean of age ratios.

2. Mean of sex ratios :

(a) Sex ratios of males per 100 females are to be calculated for all the age groups;

(b) Successive difference between succeeding and preceding sex ratios is to be worked out and summed up (ignoring signs); and

(c) Sum of difference is to be divided by total number of sex ratios. The result is the mean of sex ratio.

The United Nations Secretariat Index (UNSI) or age-sex accuracy index is worked out as follows :

UNSI = Mean deviation of male age ratio + Mean deviation of female age ratio + (3 Mean of successive differences of sex ratio).

Census age-sex data are described by United Nations as "accurate", "inaccurate" or "highly-inaccurate" depending on whether the Index is under 20, 20 to 40 or over 40.[3]

Theoretically the accuracy of the census quinquennial grouped population data can be checked up by this method. This method first indicates whether or not there is a large distortion or excess in any age group and then shows the regularities/irregularities of sex ratios and finally yields a standard result (index) either for accurate or inaccurate grouped population.

The census quinquennial age group populations of Assam for the census years 1951, 1961, 1971 and 1991 (after adjusting the population of 1951, 1961 and 1971 to the present political boundary of Assam) are checked by applying the above method.

United Nations Secretariat Indices for the Census Population of Assam 1951, 1961,1971 and 1991

The estimated values of the United Nations Secretariat Index (UNSI) are given in Tables 2.1, 2.2, 2.3 and 2.4 for the Census years 1951, 1961, 1971 and 1991 respectively. The tables show that UN Secretariat Indices are 37.65, 66.34, 53.32 and 39.98 for the respective census years. These indices show that quinquennial age group population distributors of 1961 and 1971 are 'highly inaccurate' and those of 1951 and 1991 populations 'inaccurate'. Hence, 5-year grouped population distribution of Assam are to be smoothened.

Table 2.1 : Age Accuracy Index by UN Secretarial Method : Assam: 1951

	Male			Female				
Age group	*Population*	*Age Ratio*	*Difference*	*Population*	*Age Ratio*	*Difference*	*Sex Ratio*	*Difference*
0-4	679206			652878			104.03	
5 to 9	627621	104.53	4.53	593187	107.68	7.68	105.80	1.77
10 to 14	494359	101.97	1.97	406650	89.94	10.06	121.57	15.76
15 to 19	332439	84.98	15.02	356596	96.87	3.13	93.23	28.34
20 to 24	346767	100.64	0.64	341052	100.52	0.52	101.68	8.45
25 to 29	354470	103.22	3.22	320222	102.83	2.83	110.70	9.02
30 to 34	329036	101.75	1.75	272965	102.97	2.97	120.54	9.85
35 to 39	286585	100.23	0.23	202082	95.49	4.51	141.82	21.27
40 to 44	242164	100.74	0.74	159799	98.25	1.75	151.54	9.73
45 to 49	192371	99.20	0.80	126068	98.58	1.42	152.59	1.05
50 to 54	147233	101.19	1.19	97776	99.26	0.74	150.58	2.01
55 to 59	96901	93.60	6.40	71662	97.33	2.67	135.22	15.36
60 to 64	66452	96.70	3.30	51453	98.41	1.59	129.15	6.07
65 to 69	42808	94.97	5.03	33732	97.60	2.40	126.91	2.24
70 to 74	25972			18498			140.40	13.50
75+	34389			26112				
Total	4298773		44.84	3730732		42.25		144.43
Mean			3.449			3.250		10.317

U.N.S. Index = 3.449 + 3.250 + (10.317 x 3) = 37.6501

Table 2.2 : Age Accuracy Index by UN Secretarial Method : Assam : 1961

	Male			Female				
Age group	*Population*	*Age Ratio*	*Difference*	*Population*	*Age Ratio*	*Difference*	*Sex Ratio*	*Difference*
0-4	914663			949646			96.32	
5 to 9	901910	109.00	9.00	892084	111.45	11.45	101.10	4.79
10 to 14	665755	98.52	1.48	559579	88.62	11.38	118.97	17.87
15 to 19	459615	87.61	12.39	442637	91.50	8.50	103.84	15.14
20 to 24	448514	95.19	4.81	449084	102.31	2.31	99.87	3.96
25 to 29	505416	110.54	10.54	425076	106.40	6.40	118.90	19.03
30 to 34	417802	97.46	2.54	324407	98.12	1.88	128.79	9.89
35 to 39	362877	101.78	1.78	242412	95.33	4.67	149.69	20.90
40 to 44	288958	98.09	1.91	196056	101.41	1.41	147.39	2.31
45 to 49	231939	95.37	4.63	141546	89.08	10.92	163.86	16.48
50 to 54	208714	110.67	10.67	139072	116.75	16.75	150.08	13.78
55 to 59	125143	82.07	17.93	76741	74.32	25.68	163.07	13.00
60 to 64	123607	125.28	25.28	93963	138.06	38.06	131.55	31.52
65 to 69	47233	53.97	46.03	33475	50.85	49.15	141.10	9.55
70+	91708			70050			130.92	10.18
A.N.S.	4522			3107				
Total	5798376		148.99	5038935		188.56		188.40
Mean			11.461			14.504		13.457

U.N.S. Index = 11.461 + 14.504 + (13.457 x 3) = 66.336

Table 2.3 : Age Accuracy Index by UN Secretarial Method : Assam : 1971

	Male			Female				
Age group	*Population*	*Age Ratio*	*Difference*	*Population*	*Age Ratio*	*Difference*	*Sex Ratio*	*Difference*
0-4	1242517			1254218			99.07	
5 to 9	1218261	105.42	5.42	1214471	107.18	7.18	100.31	1.25
10 to 14	1006183	105.23	5.23	930796	101.91	1.91	108.10	7.79
15 to 19	644064	87.19	12.81	594846	86.46	13.54	108.27	0.17
20 to 24	565771	95.24	4.76	538359	96.84	3.16	105.09	3.18
25 to 29	572330	105.63	5.63	534641	108.39	8.39	107.05	1.96
30 to 34	487306	95.39	4.61	406831	93.33	6.67	119.78	12.73
35 to 39	472911	106.53	6.53	366289	104.55	4.55	129.11	9.33
40 to 44	371604	96.76	3.24	277897	98.59	1.41	133.72	4.61
45 to 49	307608	98.33	1.67	201430	90.88	9.12	152.71	18.99
50 to 54	259313	105.54	5.54	185610	111.87	11.87	139.71	13.00
55 to 59	170154	86.72	13.28	110723	79.73	20.27	153.68	13.97
60 to 64	159145	116.11	16.11	120301	126.48	26.48	132.29	21.39
65 to 69	81900	62.16	37.84	54309	55.90	44.10	150.80	18.51
70+	154241			116857			131.99	18.81
A.N.S.	932			3334				
Total	7714240		122.67	6910912		158.65		145.69
Mean			9.436			12.204		10.407

U.N.S. Index = 9.4361 + 12.231 + (10.41 x 3) = 52.90

Table 2.4 : Age Accuracy Index by UN Secretarial Method : Assam : 1991

	Male			*Female*				
Age group	*Population*	*Age Ratio*	*Difference*	*Population*	*Age Ratio*	*Difference*	*Sex Ratio*	*Difference*
0-4	1522786			1489619			102.23	
5 to 9	1664132	109.02	9.02	1621948	109.70	9.70	102.60	-0.37
10 to 14	1392328	99.58	0.42	1324066	98.42	1.58	105.16	2.55
15 to 19	1138194	96.42	3.58	1090133	95.36	4.64	104.41	0.75
20 to 24	1010899	96.43	3.57	1015221	97.57	2.43	99.57	4.83
25 to 29	995859	105.73	5.73	1016294	110.73	10.73	97.99	1.59
30 to 34	818991	95.70	4.30	721874	92.47	7.53	113.45	15.46
35 to 39	752586	106.02	6.02	603728	102.88	2.88	124.66	11.20
40 to 44	557963	94.27	5.73	434903	93.62	6.38	128.30	3.64
45 to 49	464996	99.70	0.30	355057	96.60	3.40	130.96	2.67
50 to 54	376277	102.73	2.73	312731	108.39	8.39	120.32	10.64
55 to 59	257597	86.50	13.50	197790	80.64	19.36	130.24	9.92
60 to 64	259569	118.98	18.98	225265	126.78	26.78	115.23	15.01
65 to 69	137334	62.50	37.50	110001	61.66	38.34	124.85	9.62
70+	262318			199973			131.18	6.33
A.N.S.	46160			37730				
Total	11657989		111.38	10756333		142.15		93.84
Mean			8.568			10.934		6.703

U.N.S. Index = 8.568 + 10.934 + 6.703 x 3 = 39.61

Smoothening Methods of Grouped Data

A number of methods for adjusting errors in age data are available in demographic literature.

The notable general methods available for smoothening of age data are (1) Graphic method, (2) Curve fitting or mathematical method[4] developed by Carrier – Farrag, Karup-King, Newton, Arriaga, etc., (3) Summation method[5]. (4) Comparision with various types of model population method[5], and (5) The Strong or Moving Average method[6].

Kohli[7] is of the opinion that any one of these methods is good enough for those countries where age groups of population do not exhibit any wide discrepancy. But in population, where age returns are seriously distorted, as in the case of India, direct treatment of unadjusted age data by any of the methods cannot be expected to yield satisfactory results. These statistical methods are designed to delimit large fluctuations, which mask the true distribution. However, they may fail to remove large systematic irregularities. It is for this reason that the International Institute of Population Studies (IIPS), Bombay has recently developed a smoothening method which first takes care of large omission or excess in quinquennial age group oy making age ratios nearly 100, and then applies summation formula to obtain single year smooth population distribution.[8] This method has been extensively used by many Asian countries, as it is considered suitable and appropriate for removing serious distortion in age returns.[9] But in our study only 5-year age grouped smoothened populations are required. Hence it does not call for the application of summation formula mentioned above. Srinivasan is of opinion that Moving Average method is routinely used in the smoothening of Indian census data.[10] In this method the corrected population size at any age (i) is considered to be equal to the average of the three observed values at adjacent ages **i-1, i, i+1**. The corrected population in the age group **Pi** would be expressed as follows-[11]

$$\textbf{Pi (corrected population)} = (P_{i-1} + P_i + P_{i+1}) / 3$$

"In severe cases of errors in reporting of age where it is felt that the errors could spill over to the adjacent ages, a five-year moving average can be used".[12] By following these two smoothening methods viz, method of Moving Average and method developed by IIPS, Bombay, another method is developed termed as Grouped Age Ratio Adjusted Multiplier. In this method 5 year grouped population data are first smoothened by applying both Moving Average method and then re-smoothened by applying 'Grouped Age Ratio Multiplier method, so that age ratios become close to 100. The 5-year grouped populations of Assam for the census years 1951, 1961, 1971 and 1991 are smoothened by applying Moving Average and Age Ratio Adjusted Multiplier methods. But before doing so, a few observations have been made on the United Nations Secretariat Index and age ratios of 5-year age grouped population of Assam, for the respective years.

Some Theoretical Aspects and Primary Observations on Age Ratios

It is a well-known and established fact that smoothened quinquennial age group population by any method will ultimately yield two series of age ratios (male and female), the percentage values of which are close to 100 and a systematic arrangement of sex ratios giving UNSI within the prescribed limit of below 20. However, the United Nations have suggested a standard age ratio score of 2.6 for male and 2.4 for female with a sex ratio score of 1.5, resulting in joint score of 9.5 based on Swedish population.[14] It is worth mentioning that the joint score of 9.5 can be taken as standard, if there is no heavy migration (in or out) and heavy mortality in the age distributions.

The theoreticians of any smoothening method assume that excepting extreme fluctuations in past birth, deaths or migration, the three age groups should form a nearly linear series, the age ratios of which approximating 100.[15] The age ratio indicates whether an age group is under-enumerated or over-enumerated. Age ratio appreciably below and above 100 indicates under-enumeration and over-enumeration respectively. On the other hand the under-enumeration and over-enumeration may be assumed to be really genuine if there are no migrations and heavy deaths. However, genuineness of age ratio, appreciably above 100, can be checked whether it is due to in-migration or over-enumeration. It is generally believed that in-migration may influence the age groups like 20-24, 25-29, and 30-34. If age ratios in these groups are found, say, around 110 then these may commonly be treated as due to in-migration as over-enumeration in all these three age groups is not possible.

If the age ratios of the age groups preceding and succeeding the age group of 20-24 or 25-29 are found to be approximately 100, and the age ratio of age group 20-24 or 25-29 is far above 100 then it can be surmised that the age group 20-24 or 25-29 is influenced by in-migration because there is less chance of over-enumeration in this age group, as other preceding and succeeding age groups are saturated by age ratios close to 100. However, even if the age ratios in all the age groups are found to be nearly 100, this does not necessarily preclude the possibility of migration in the age groups owing to the following reasons.

(a) The grouped populations in a census, from the age group 10-14 onwards depend on their 'base population' or 'cohort' of previous the census. (The population of each age group of a census is termed as cohort for the next census age group advanced by 10 years, and the grouped populations in the next census, operated after 10 years, advanced by 10 years to the cohorts are termed as 'survivors'). Generally it is believed that cohort, i.e., initial population has a tendency to decrease by a certain proportion (as per mortality rate). Therefore, if there is no migration, the survivor age group populations will always be lower than those of cohort age group populations. From this common postulate, it can be assumed that if the age ratio in all age groups, in two consecutive censuses were close to 100, and if the 'survivors' age group populations were higher than their cohort age groups populations, then in spite of the age ratios being close to 100 in all age groups, there are in-migrants in all the age groups except in the age groups 0-4 and 5-9 in the succeeding census because these age groups have no cohorts but births. On the contrary it could again be assumed that if age ratio of cohorts age groups is close to 100, and age ratio of survivors age group populations in the successive census is not close to 100 and if survivors age groups populations are substantially higher than those of the 'cohorts' age groups population in a selective age group, say, between 15-19 and 35-39, then in spite of the distorted age ratios in these age groups (15-19 to 35-39), there are in-migrants in all these age groups. And finally if both the age ratios, viz. cohorts, age groups populations and survivors', age groups populations are distorted, and if the survivors age groups populations are higher either in selective age groups (15-19 to 35-39) or in all age groups, there are also chances of in-migration, because in no case, 'survivors' can be higher than the cohorts in all age groups. (Table 2.5 presents the cohorts and survivors with their age ratios for a few selective age groups).

(b) If the age ratios of both the censuses are close to 100, and if the number of 'survivors' in the next census is substantially lower than that of the cohorts, there is less chance of in-migration, although it does not rule out in-migration altogether. There may be in-migration or out-migration, because actual number of survivors is a product of cohorts and life table survival rates.

Table 2.5 : Cohort and Survivor of a few Select Age Groups

Male					
		1951		*1961*	
Age Group	*Population*	*Age ratio*	*Age Group*	*Population*	*Age ratio*
15-19	332439	84.98	25-29	505416	110.54
20-24	346767	100.60	30-34	417802	97.46
25-29	3544470	103.2	35-39	362877	101.78
Female					
10-14	406650	89.94	20-24	449087	102.3
15-19	356596	96.87	25-29	425076	106.4
Male					
1961	1971				
0-4	914663	-	10-14	106183	105.2
5-9	901910	109.00	15-19	64404	87.17
15-19	459615	87.61	25-29	572330	105.6
20-24	448514	95.19	30-34	487306	95.39
Female					
15-19	442637	91.5	25-29	534641	108.4
20-24	449084	102.2	30-34	406831	93.33
25-29	425076	106.4	35-39	366289	104.6
Male					
1971	1991				
15-19	644064	87.10	35-39	752586	106.00
Female					
15-19	594846	86.46	35-39	603728	102.88

Derived from Tables. 2.1, 2.2, 2.3 and 2.4

Compensation of Age Ratios

(a) If cohorts and survivors (as a product of cohort and survival ratio) indicate that there is substantial in-migration in the age groups, say, 20-24, 25-29 and 30-34 and if the age ratios of these three age groups are 95.19.90, 110.54 and 97.46 respectively, (Table 2.2) then it can be inferred that there is either heavy in-migration in the age group 25-29. Alternatively, age ratio of 110.54 in the age group 25-29 may be the result of clustering of population in the age groups 20-24 and 30-34 respectively, at the expense of the age ratio of 89 and 96 of the respective groups.

(b) Alternatively, if cohorts and survivors indicate that there is no in-migration in the age groups, say, 20-24, 25-29 and 30-34, and if the age ratios of the respective age groups are similar to those mentioned in (a) above, then it can be inferred that the age ratio of the age has compensated for the lower age ratio of 20-24 and 30-34 age groups.

The above theoretical discussion may be summarized as follows -

1. Generally quinquennial age groups are smoother than single year age data and found naturally in a decreasing order. Theoretically the mean of three consecutive age group populations should be approximately equal to that of the middle age group of three consecutive age groups. The age ratio of three consecutive age groups should be close to 100 if there is no heavy migration (in or out) or deaths;

2. Age ratio appreciably below and above 100 could be treated as under-enumeration and over-enumeration respectively, if other things remain constant;

3. Age ratio appreciably below and above 100 could be treated as the influence of migration (out and in respectively), if other things remain constant;

4. Age ratio in a particular age group appreciably below 100 does not necessarily mean that there is out-migration, if 'cohort' of the previous census is reasonably higher than this particular age group;

5. Age ratio of 110, in an age group like 25-29, does not necessarily mean that there is in-migration in that age group, it may just compensate for the lower age ratios of the preceding and succeeding age groups;

6. Even if age ratios in all groups are close to 100, it does not rule out the possibilities of in-migration, particularly if the survivors in the 'linked' age groups are higher than the cohort population in the preceding census;

7. Age ratios may have some tendency to go down from 100 either in very young age or in extreme old age, because of high mortality rates;

8. Even after having a reasonably standard smoothening, there may be age ratio like 103 if other things do not remain constant (because of the presence of migration); and

9. Misstatement of age is common to both indigenous and migrant population.

Keeping the above in mind the following observations may be made with respect to census population of Assam for the years 1951, 1961, 1971 and 1991.

1951 Census Population

In 1951 census, 1286624 persons were tabulated as immigrants[16] (1344003 for the then political boundary of Assam).[17] In this study it has been assumed that these 12,86,624 persons constituted a part of the population of Assam in 1951. Further it has been assumed that the immigrants by quinquennial age groups are distributed in percentage terms more or less close to that of indigenous population, because these are push-factor-oriented migrants (where family as a whole had migrated). As a consequence, 1951 census age groups ratios show an arrangement of age ratios almost close to 100, except in a few age groups. Therefore it can be assumed that all those in-migrants were distributed in all the age groups similar to the indigenous population. Observing the age groups population of 1951, Chari remarks, "There are also reasons to believe, though with no evidence to support, that this population transfer was by and large families so that its effect on the age distribution will be distributed equally over all the age groups".[18] However, the possibility of misreporting of age either by indigenous or by migrant population cannot be ruled out. The following observations may be made with regards to the census 5-year grouped population of 1951.

1951 Male Age Ratio

1. The male mean age ratio of census population is found to be 3.4 (Table 2.1). As the standard male age ratio's upper limit is 2.6, therefore mean male age ratio mentioned above can be taken as more or less satisfactory.

2. Age ratios of the initial age-groups starting from 5-9 to 20-24 are 104.3, 102.0, 84.98 and 100.6 respectively. The age ratios in the succeeding age groups starting from 20-24 to 50-54, are almost close to 100 except in age groups 25-29 (103) and 30-34 (102). As the age ratios up to the age group 50-54 are around 100 in most of the age groups, (may be with migrants), therefore significantly low age ratio of 84.98 in age group 15-19 may be treated as under-enumeration. There is a probability of under-enumeration in the age group 0-4 also, as the age ratio of its succeeding age groups (i.e. 5-9 and 10-14) are 104.5 and 102.0 respectively. Generally the age ratio in the age group 5-9 should be just below 100 (say 99 or 98) due to high rate of child mortality. It has again

be observed that there is always a marked deficit in the age group 0-4.[19] Census of India 1971 observed, 'the cohort of survivors in the age 10-14 in 1971 is larger than the original cohort of persons aged 0-4 in 1961 which is also suggestive of heavy under-enumeration in the very younger ages 0-4'.[20] But it is worth mentioning that rate of under-enumeration in age 0-4 is appreciably higher in male than that of female, as the original cohorts of female (0-4 age group) is always higher than those of survivors age group (10-14) in the next census. The census populations (India) of these two age groups, presented by Table 2.6., substantiate this point.

Table 2.6 : Original Survivors and Cohort, India 1951, 1961 and 1971

(in thousand)

Year	*Age Groups*	*Population*	*Year*	*Age Groups*	*Population*
Male					
1951	0-4	24582	1961	10-14	26280
1961	0-4	33105	1971	10-14	36033
Female					
1951	0-4	24340	1961	10-14	23043
1961	0-4	32944	1971	10-14	31891

Source : For 1951 and 1961, K.L. Kohli, *Mortality in India, op. cit*, pp. 148-150 and for 1971 *Census of India* 1971, Paper 2, p. 8

1951 Female Age Ratio

1. Female mean age ratio of 3.24 as compared to standard female mean age ratio of 2.4, (Table 2.1) is more or less satisfactory. However, female age ratios are more distorted than those of male age ratios.

2. Population in the age group 5-9 is an over-enumeration compared to that of the age group 10-14, as the age ratio in this age group (10-14) is 89.94. The age ratio in the age group 15-19 is also a deficit one (96.87) and age ratio in the age groups 20-24, 25-29, 30-34 and 35-39 are 100.5, 102.8, 103.0, and 95.49 respectively. Age ratio of 103 in the age group 30-34 may be a compensation for the age group 35-39 where age ratio is 95.49. The age ratios, beyond the age group 40-44 are more or less satisfactory as these are close to 100.

1951 Sex Ratio

Theoretically, the mean of successive difference of sex ratios in a migration free and sudden heavy death free population should be 1.5.

But against this standard value, 1951 population gives a mean of successive difference of sex ratio equal to 10.32. This indicates that sex ratios are severely distorted. The heavy distortion of sex ratios is observed in all the age groups from 5-9 to 25-29. One of the reasons for this distortion is the fluctuations of age ratios. Table 2.1 shows that sex ratios in age groups 10-14, 15-19, 20-24, 25-29 and 35-39 are 121.57, 93.23, 101.68, 110.7, and 120.54 respectively. This indicates larger number of females in the age groups 10-14, 20-24 and 25-29. Observing the similar situation in the census population of India for 1971, (where population could be assumed as 'closed') Chari[21] remarks, "despite of the masculinity of the population with males exceeding females as much as by 20 million, females are observed to be more in number than males at the ages 20, 24, 25, 28 and 30 with the result that in the age-groups 20-24 and 25-29 the females outnumber males".

1951 Joint Score

United Nations Secretariat Index or age ratio sex ratio joint score for 1951 population is found to be 37.65 (Table 2.1). Theoretically the joint score should be below 20 to yield an accurate age distribution. Therefore 1951 age groups population needs smoothening.

1961 Census Age Data

The male and female mean age ratios 11.46 and 14.50 respectively as compared to standard age ratios of male (2.6) and female (2.4) are not at all satisfactory. The mean of successive difference of sex ratio of 13.46, as compared to standard mean sex ratio of 1.5, indicates heavy distortion in sex ratios. The joint score 66.34 again shows high inaccuracy of arrangement of grouped age data of 1961 census.

Table 2.2 shows that there is not even a single age ratio that is close to 100, either for male or female. Male age ratio of 110.54 in the age group 25-29 could be taken as a compensation for the age groups 20-24 and 30-34. Age ratios of age group 5-9 for both male (109) and female (111.4) indicate over-enumeration, as their succeeding age ratio are found below 100. Age ratios of 87.61 male in the age group 15-19 and that of female (88.62) in the age group 10-14 indicate marked under-enumeration.

Sex ratios in the age groups 0-4 and 20-24 show 96.32 and 99.87 males per 100 females respectively. On the other hand sex ratios in all other age groups are dominated by male ranging from 101 to 163 males per 100 females. The sudden ups and downs in the sex ratios, up to the age group 30-34 and then sharp increase in the age group 35-39 may be explained in terms of distorted age ratios of both male and female, as it has been observed that (Table 2.2) sex ratios tend to increase or decrease sharply where there is a substantial gap between age ratios of male and female. If the age ratios for both male and female were close to 100, then these sudden upheavals in sex ratios would not have been seen.

1971 Census Age Data

1971 Census age data of quinquennial age groups (Table 3.3) are similar to those of 1961 age data. The male and female mean age ratios of 9.43 and 12.20 respectively indicate heavy distortion in the age ratios. For instance male age ratios in the age groups 5-9, 10-14, 25-29, 35-39, 50-54 and 60-64 are found to be 105.4, 105.2, 105.6, 106.5, 105.5 and 116.1 respectively and the age ratios in the almost all alternate age groups 15-19, 20-24, 30-34, 40-44, 55-59 and 65-69 are found to be 87.19, 95.24, 95.39, 96.76, 86.72, and 62.16 respectively. (The similar pattern of age ratio distribution is observed in female age ratios also). This indicates that age ratio beyond 100 in one age group is a compensation for the age ratio below 100 of the alternate age group. It will be absurd to infer that heavy in-migration in one age group is followed by heavy out migration in alternate age group, nor the fluctuation in the age ratios in alternative age groups can be satisfactorily explained in terms of mortality rates. It may, therefore, be concluded that the ups and downs in age ratio are either resulting from misstatement of age either by indigenous or by migrant populations, or by both.

The sex ratio, except in the age group 0-4 indicates more males than females. The mean of successive difference of sex ratios 10.41 indicates the lack of smoothness of the sex ratio.

The overall, age-sex accuracy index of 52.9 indicates the need of smoothening the grouped population age data of 1961 census.

1991 Census Age Data

The census grouped age data of 1991 is a slight improvement over the grouped age data of 1961 and 1971, as its 'joint-score' 39.61 is not 'highly-inaccurate' but 'simply inaccurate'. Improvement is noticeable as there is no age ratio like 88 between age groups 5-9 and 50-54. However, such improvements are not observed in the age group above 50-54, when the age ratios, for both males and females, are found fluctuating between 62.5 and 119 (male) and 61.66 and 126.78 (female).

Census Age Data : Overall Observations

To summarize, age ratios since 1951 in the age group 5-9 exceed by 4.5 to 11.45 percentage the standard age-ratio of 100 and in most cases age ratios either in the age group 10-14 or 15-19 show a marked deficit (Table 2.7). It has also been observed that except in 1951 census, in most cases the age ratio of age groups 20-24 and 30-34 indicate marked deficit, and age ratio in the age group 25-29 is 'over balanced'. These form a broad hollow age group 10-34 (Table 2.7). Observing this situation in most of the low income countries, Coale and Hoover[22] point out that the age span 10-30 shows a marked deficit. Jain[23] also makes a similar statement on the India's census age data of 1951. Zachariah[24] in a study of internal migration finds out a hollow age distribution in the Censuses of 1901, 1911, and 1921. According to the United Nations this hollow in the age span is due mostly to misstatement of age[25].

Table 2.7: Age Ratio in the Age Groups 10-14 to 30-34

Age Groups	*1951*		*1961*		*1971*		*1991*	
	Male	*Female*	*Male*	*Female*	*Male*	*Female*	*Male*	*Female*
5-9	104.5	107.7	109.0	111.4	105.4	107.2	109.0	109.7
10-14	102.2	89.9	98.5	88.6	105.4	101.9	99.6	98.4
15-19	85.0	96.9	87.6	91.5	87.2	86.5	96.4	95.4
20-24	100.6	100.5	95.2	102.3	95.2	96.8	96.4	97.6
25-29	103.2	102.8	110.5	106.4	105.6	108.4	105.7	110.7
30-34	101.8	103.0	97.5	98.1	95.4	93.3	95.7	92.9

Smoothening of Census Grouped Age Data

The Principle of Grouped Age Ratio Adjusted Multiplier (GARAM)

In a linear series the sum of the first and third digits is equal to double of the second digit. If the linear series is arranged as -

10, 11, 12, ... or 12, 11, 10, ...

then the sum of the first and third digits of this series will be equal to 22 (i.e. 10 + 12 = 22 or 12 + 10 = 22), and this sum is just equal to double of the second digit (i.e. 11 X 2 = 22). If the first, second and third digits are $\mathbf{P_1}$, $\mathbf{P_2}$ and $\mathbf{P_3}$ respectively, then the relation between the digits in a linear series can be expressed in terms of equation as follows –

$$P_1 + P_3 = 2P_2 \qquad \text{.......... (1)}$$

$$\text{Or} \quad P_3 = 2P_2 - P_1 \qquad \text{.......... (2)}$$

Equation (2) implies that if first and second digits are known, then the third digit can be easily worked out.

If the symbols $\mathbf{P_1}$, $\mathbf{P_2}$ and $\mathbf{P_3}$ stand for the population figures of three consecutive age groups, and if the population figures of $\mathbf{P_1}$ and $\mathbf{P_2}$ could be scientifically estimated, then the expected figure of $\mathbf{P_3}$ (population of third age group) can be worked out with equation (2).

The Co-efficient of P_2 of equation (2) i.e. 2 is the multiplier, the value of which may not remain fixed. The equation can be rewritten as follows –

$$\mathbf{P_3 = (Multiplier \times P_2) - P_1} \quad \ldots\ldots\ldots \quad (3)$$

The central value of multiplier is 2 and it may vary between 1.92 and 2.15 (Table 2.8). The central value of multiplier being equal to 2 means it needs twice population in the second age group (of three consecutive age groups population) to have a perfectly smooth population in the third age group. For example if population $\mathbf{P_1}$ and $\mathbf{P_2}$ for the first and second age groups are 100 and 90 respectively then population $\mathbf{P_3}$ in the third age group would be

$$\mathbf{P_3 = (Multiplier \times P_2) - P_1}$$

$$\mathbf{P_3 = 90 \times 2 - 100 = 80}$$

Thus the age ratio of these three consecutive age groups will be as–

$$\textbf{Age Ratio} = \frac{P_1}{(P_1 + P_2 + P_3)/3} \times 100 = \frac{9.0}{(100 + 90 + 80)/3} \times 100$$

$$= \mathbf{90 / 90 \times 100 = 100}$$

It is not possible to get age ratios equal to 100 in all the age groups. If these are so worked out (i.e., age ratios equal to 100), then the total population of the census will be saturated say within ten age groups, or it will give such a population figure in each age group which is not at all close to census expected population of that age group (census expected population means the mean of three consecutive original census age group population). Therefore, 'Age Ratio Adjustment Multiplier' varies, more accurately within 2.07 to 1.98 (Set – A) in the middle age groups, 2.07 to 2.15 (Set – B) in old age groups, say above 65, and 1.97 to 1.92 (Set – C) in those age groups where it deems fit to the original census population. The values of Age Ratios Adjustment Multiplier and their related age ratios to each multiplier are given in Table 2.8.

Table 2.8 : Age Ratio Adjusted Multiplier and its Related Age Ratios

Set – A		*Set – B*		*Set- C*	
Multiplier	*Age Ratio*	*Multiplier*	*Age Ratio*	*Multiplier*	*Age Ratio*
1.98	100.67	2.07	97.72	1.97	101.01
1.99	100.33	2.08	97.40	1.96	101.35
2.00	100.00	2.09	97.09	1.95	101.69
2.01	99.67	2.10	96.77	1.94	102.03
2.02	99.34	2.11	96.46	1.93	102.37
2.03	99.01	2.12	96.15	1.92	102.74
2.04	98.68	2.13	95.85		
2.05	98.36	2.14	95.54		
2.06	98.04	2.15	95.24		
2.07	97.72				

Application of Age Ratio Adjusted Multiplier to Census Grouped Population

To apply grouped population age ratio adjusted multiplier, reasonably accurate populations of two consecutive age groups are required. The populations of two consecutive age groups can be said to be reasonably accurate or smooth if the age ratio of the two consecutive age groups is nearing 100. It is because, any two consecutive age ratios nearing 100 indicate that in these age groups populations are smoothly arranged and from these two age group populations, the population of preceding and succeeding age groups can be smoothly worked out by applying age ratio multiplier. But unfortunately in the census populations of Assam, except for 1951, there are no such population age groups which, consecutively give the age ratio close to 100 at least for two consecutive age groups. In this situation it is necessary to work out two reasonably accurate (smooth) age group populations from the original census population. These two age group populations can be worked out by applying Moving Average method. This method implies that the fluctuation of grouped population can be smoothened by taking either three-year or five-year moving average. By following this method two consecutively smooth grouped populations are work out as follows [26]–

If P_i, P_{ii}, P_{iii}, P_{iv}, and P_v are the original census population of age groups 1st, 2nd, 3rd, 4th and 5th respectively, then the mean of population of first three age groups (P_1) and second three age groups (P_2) will be as follows –

$$P_1 = (P_i + P_{ii} + P_{iii}) / 3$$
$$P_2 = (P_{ii} + P_{iii} + P_{iv}) / 3$$

Thus the expected smooth population (EP_3) in the next age group would be

$$EP_3 = (\text{Multiplier x } P_2) - P_1$$

Any of the multiplier can be applied to find the next age group population, (as specified in Table 2.8) but enough precaution is to be taken to work out such a population figure in the next age group which should be closer to or almost equal to the mean of the three consecutive age group original census populations. For example, the probable population in the age group 15-19 should be closer to the mean of the census original population of the age groups 10-14, 15-19 and 20-24. However, exception may be there. As shown in Table 2.7, at times, there may be marked deficit in the consecutive age ratios in the original census population. In such a case, the expected population in the age group, say, 15-19 can be assumed as close to the general mean between the mean of three consecutive age group and five consecutive age group populations around the age group 15-19. If both are not satisfactory then any of the multipliers of Set-A of Table 2.8 is to be applied. But in most of the age groups, it has been observed that the expected smooth population in a particular age group, except below age 5 and age over 65 is within the boundary of either the mean of three consecutive age groups or the mean of five consecutive age groups of original census populations.

The method of smoothening quinquennial age group population as explained in the above paragraph gives the grouped population from the age group 5-9 onwards, because it requires three age group populations to work out the mean population of the any age group. But it is not possible to estimate 0-4 group population by averaging three consecutive age groups populations, population figures start from the age group 0-4. The simplest method to work out 0-4 age group population is the extrapolation of 10-14 and 5-9 age group populations. The extrapolation must be done in such a way that the age ratio between the age groups 0-4, 5-9 and 10-14 becomes close to 100.

Another method[27] to estimate 0-4 age group population is-

$$P_{0-4} = \text{Birth}_{(5\,yr)} - \text{Death}_{(0-4)} \pm \text{Migration}_{(0-4)}$$

Where P_{0-4} is population in the 0-4 age group, $\text{Birth}_{(5\,yr)}$ is total number of births in the last five years, $\text{Death}_{(0-4)}$ is the number of deaths in the age group 0-4 and migration (0-4) is the number of migrants (in or out) in 0-4 age group. This method is applicable to those areas or states where data on migration are accurately recorded/maintained. But in a state like Assam where age specific birth place statistics (from which migration figures are estimated) are unreliable[28], the method does not yield accurate results.

Smoothening

1. From the grouped original population age group 5-9 population is worked out as the mean of three consecutive age groups around 5-9 (Moving Average Method) .

2. The original census population of the age group 10-14 shows a marked deficit in most of the censuses. Therefore the mean population of age group 10-14 is worked out as the mean of either three consecutive age group population or five consecutive age group population, around the age group 10-14. The population of the age group 10-14 is in such a way adjusted, so that difference between multiplier times (multiplier of Set-A) 10-14 age group population and 5-9 age group population (mean of three consecutive age groups around age 5-9) becomes close to the mean of three or five consecutive age groups population around the age group 10-14, i.e., becomes near to expected population in the age group 15-19. Symbolically this relation is as follows

$$\mathbf{EX\ P_{15\text{-}19} = (X\ P_{10\text{-}14}\ x\ Multiplier) - X\ P_{5\text{-}9}}$$

Where $\mathbf{EXP_{15\text{-}19}}$ is the expected mean population in the age group 15-19, and $\mathbf{XP_{10\text{-}14}}$ and $\mathbf{XP_{5\text{-}9}}$ are the mean populations of age groups 10-14 (three or five consecutive age groups around 10-14 age group) and 5-9 (three consecutive age groups around age group 5-9) respectively.

Smoothening of Age group population up to age groups 55-59

The populations of the age groups 15-19 to 55-59 (more specifically the age group up to 45-49) are estimated by applying age ratio adjusted multiplier. The expected population in any age group is assumed to be equal to the mean of three or five consecutive age group populations.

Age group population above 60

There is a general tendency to overstate one's age in old age, which increases with the increase in age. This is termed by some as 'ageing'. It has been observed that smooth population in the broad age group 60 + is generally lower than of that of original census population. The smoothened population of India in 1971 is 27.45% lower than that of original unsmoothened population[29]. Therefore the age group populations of ages above 60 are smoothened by applying age ratio adjusted multiplier of Set

B and Set C (Multipliers values of Set C imply the existence of high mortality rates).

Sex Ratio

There is a regularity in the change of sex ratio from one age group to another age group. If there is no heavy male migration (in or out) no heavy war deaths, then sex ratio falls gradually throughout the life.[30] On the contrary if there is heavy maternal death, sex ratio declines upto the age 50 and then gently increases with age. But it is difficult to maintain both i.e., age ratio near to 100 and regularity of sex ratio. It is generally assumed that if age ratios are properly arranged then the sex ratios will be accordingly arranged.

Adjustment of total population

Any deviation (termed as residue) in the total smoothened population from the original census total needs adjustment, i.e. total of smoothened population must be equal to the original census total. It is found that total smoothened population of the quinquennial age groups varies slightly from the total original census population. Therefore smoothened grouped populations are adjusted to the original census total. The adjustments are made as follows :

1. The ratio between total smoothened population and total original population is worked out. This ratio is applied to the smoothened populations of each age groups. The sum of the products of ratio (between total smoothed and original total) and smoothened population in each age group becomes equal to the original census total.

Age Ratio-Sex Ratio Joint Score

The smoothened populations for the census years 1951, 1961, 1971, and 1991 are given in Tables 2.10, 2.11, 2.12 and 2.13 respectively. The joint score or United Nations Secretariat Index for the years are as follows:

Table 2.9 : Joint Score (UNSI) for years 1951, 1961, 1971 and 1991

1951	7.94
1961	12.72
1971	14.15
1991	12.89

U.N. Secretariat indices indicate that smoothening of quinquennial age group populations are satisfactory, as these are within the limit of below 20.

Table 2.10 : Age Accuracy Index by UN Secretarial Method : Assam: 1951

	Male			Female				
Age group	*Population*	*Age.Ratio*	*Difference*	*Population*	*Age Ratio*	*Difference*	*Sex Ratio*	*Difference*
0-4	695812			657974			105.75	
5 to 9	585239	99.46	0.54	549758	100.00	0.00	106.45	0.70
10 to 14	484160	98.36	1.64	441538	97.89	2.11	109.65	3.20
15 to 19	407289	98.36	1.64	361845	98.35	1.65	112.56	2.91
20 to 24	350782	98.36	1.64	300330	97.93	2.07	116.80	4.24
25 to 29	311814	98.68	1.32	257816	98.03	1.97	120.94	4.15
30 to 34	285318	100.00	0.00	230852	99.51	0.49	123.59	2.65
35 to 39	258784	100.72	0.72	207333	100.61	0.61	124.82	1.22
40 to 44	226721	100.67	0.67	180014	100.64	0.64	125.95	1.13
45 to 49	190150	100.44	0.44	149250	100.00	0.00	127.40	1.46
50 to 54	151069	99.26	0.74	118486	99.33	0.67	127.50	0.10
55 to 59	115351	97.11	2.89	90118	97.13	2.87	128.00	0.50
60 to 64	89915	98.69	1.31	69737	98.10	1.90	128.93	0.93
65 to 69	68051	98.58	1.42	53415	98.88	1.12	127.40	1.53
70 to 74	49127			38913			126.25	1.15
75+	29191			23353				
Total	4298773		14.95	3730732		16.11		25.87
Mean			1.150			1.239		1.848

U.N.S. Index = 1.150 + 1.239 + (1.848 x 3) = 7.94

Table 2.11: Age Accuracy Index by UN Secretarial Method : Assam : 1961

	Male			*Female*				
Age group	*Population*	*Age Ratio*	*Dif.*	*Population*	*Age Ratio*	*Dif.*	*Sex Ratio*	*Dif.*
0-4	923838			921101			100.30	
5 to 9	782510	98.31	1.69	740146	97.13	2.87	105.72	5.43
10 to 14	681432	98.63	1.37	624762	98.21	1.79	109.07	3.35
15 to 19	608651	99.89	0.11	543509	99.98	0.02	111.99	2.91
20 to 24	537844	100.00	0.00	462565	100.00	0.00	116.27	4.29
25 to 29	467037	100.00	0.00	381621	100.00	0.00	122.38	6.11
30 to 34	396230	100.00	0.00	300677	97.07	2.93	131.78	9.40
35 to 39	325423	98.66	1.34	246973	98.35	1.65	131.76	0.01
40 to 44	267925	97.93	2.07	205718	98.67	1.33	130.24	1.53
45 to 49	227381	99.74	0.26	172771	100.00	0.00	131.61	1.37
50 to 54	188594	100.74	0.74	139824	100.00	0.00	134.88	3.27
55 to 59	145666	99.82	0.18	106877	99.38	0.62	136.29	1.41
60 to 64	103539	98.63	1.37	75930	97.61	2.39	136.36	0.07
65 to 69	65742	94.20	5.80	50566	96.09	3.91	130.01	6.35
70 to 74	40093			31369			127.81	2.20
75+	36471			34544				
Total	5798376		14.92	5038953		17.51		47.69
Mean			1.148			1.347		3.407

U.N.S. Index = 1.148 + 1.347 + (3.407 x 3) = 12.715

Table 2.12 : Age Accuracy Index by UN Secretarial Method : Assam : 1971

	Male			*Female*				
Age group	*Population*	*Age Ratio*	*Dif.*	*Population*	*Age Ratio*	*Dif.*	*Sex Ratio*	*Dif.*
0-4	1213550			1211698			100.15	
5 to 9	1048138	100.02	-0.02	1044274	100.98	0.98	100.37	0.22
10 to 14	882090	97.30	2.70	846406	97.05	2.95	104.22	3.85
15 to 19	789561	99.38	0.62	725810	99.23	0.77	108.78	4.57
20 to 24	711833	100.18	0.18	622028	98.96	1.04	114.44	5.65
25 to 29	630186	100.27	0.27	537867	100.00	0.00	117.16	2.73
30 to 34	543414	99.38	0.62	453706	100.00	0.00	119.77	2.61
35 to 39	466892	100.37	0.37	369545	99.38	0.62	126.34	6.57
40 to 44	385245	100.00	0.00	292303	98.64	1.36	131.80	5.45
45 to 49	303598	99.05	0.95	227153	96.84	3.16	133.65	1.86
50 to 54	230710	96.56	3.44	184232	99.07	0.93	125.23	8.43
55 to 59	182451	99.56	0.44	146484	100.12	-0.12	124.55	0.67
60 to 64	136615	100.01	0.01	108209	100.00	0.00	126.25	1.70
65 to 69	90749	96.77	3.23	69934	96.57	3.43	129.76	3.51
70 to 74	53957			39105			137.98	8.22
75+	44951			32158				
Total	7713940		12.81	6910912		15.12		56.03
Mean			0.986			1.163		4.002

U.N.S. Index = 0.986 + 1.163 + (4.002 x 3) = 14.15

Table 2.13 : Age Accuracy Index by UN Secretarial Method : Assam : 1991

	Male			Female				
Age group	*Population*	*Age Ratio*	*Dif.*	*Population*	*Age Ratio*	*Dif.*	*Sex Ratio*	*Dif.*
0-4	1516538			1404691			107.96	
5 to 9	1374147	99.93	0.07	1262910	97.91	2.09	108.81	0.85
10 to 14	1234790	98.36	1.64	1202181	100.05	0.05	102.71	6.10
15 to 19	1157283	98.40	1.60	1139730	98.88	1.12	101.54	1.17
20 to 24	1136106	102.99	2.99	1116086	102.84	2.84	101.79	0.25
25 to 29	1015875	100.74	0.74	1000023	102.56	2.56	101.59	0.21
30 to 34	873222	99.03	0.97	809153	98.29	1.71	107.92	6.33
35 to 39	756135	98.88	1.12	660408	97.99	2.01	114.50	6.58
40 to 44	664783	100.52	0.52	552366	98.78	1.22	120.35	5.86
45 to 49	563058	100.62	0.62	464867	99.91	0.09	121.12	0.77
50 to 54	450978	99.34	0.66	378582	100.36	0.36	119.12	2.00
55 to 59	347945	99.66	0.34	288206	99.57	0.43	120.73	1.60
60 to 64	248522	99.20	0.80	201552	98.19	1.81	123.30	2.58
65 to 69	155117	96.01	3.99	126067	94.37	5.63	123.04	0.26
70 to 74	81041			73148			110.79	12.25
75+	82449			76363				
Total	11657989		16.07	10756333		21.93		46.81
Mean			1.236			1.687		3.343

U.N.S. Index = 1.236 + 1.687 + (3.343 X 3) = 12.95

References

1. K. Srinivasan, *Basic Demographic Techniques and Applications*, Sage Publication, New Delhi, 1998, p. 166.

2. H. S. Shryock, *et al. Methods and Materials of Demography, op. cit*, p. 115.

3. *ibid*. p126

4. K.L. Kohli, *Mortality in India*, op cit., p 40

5. H.S. Shyrock , *et al.*, *Methods and Materials of Demography op cit.*, p127

6. K.Srinivasan, *Basic Demographic Techniques and Applications, op cit.*, p. 167

7. K.L. Kohli, *Mortality in India*, op cit., p.40

8. *ibid*, p. 41

9. S.L.N. Rao, 'Age Distribution and Life Table Development', in K.L. Kohli, *Mortality in India, op cit*. p. 41

10. K. Srinivasan, *Basic Demographic Techniques and Applications*, op. cit, p. 169.

11. *ibid*, p. 168

12. *ibid*, p. 169

13. K.L. Kohli, *Mortality in India, op cit*, p. 148-211

14. United Nations : "Accuracy Test for Census Age Distributions Tabulated in Five Year and Ten Year Groups", *Population Bulletin*, No. 2, Oct. 1952, New York, UN, 1953, p 61

15. H. S. Shyrock, *et. al. Methods and Materials of Demography, op. cit.*, p. 124

16. *Census of India 1971, Assam, General Report*, p. 60

17. *ibid*, p. 10

18. R. B. Chari , *Census of India*, Paper 206, 1974, p. 2

19. K. L. Kohli, *Mortality in India ,op cit*, p. 18

20. *Census of India 1971*, Series I, India Paper 2 of 1974. p. 2

21 R.B. Chari , *Census of India 1971*, Paper 2 of 1974, *op. cit.* p. 2

22. A.J. Coale, and Hoover E.M., *Population Growth and Economic Development in Low Income Countries*, Princeton, University Press, 1958, p. 347

23. S.P. Jain, *Census of India 1951*, Paper 2 of 1954, Life Table, 1951, p. 15

24. K.C., Zachariah, *A Historical Study of Internal Migration in the Indian Sub-Continent*, 1930-31, Bombay Asia Publishing House, 1964, p. 29

25. United Nations' *Methods of Estimating Basic Demographic Measures from Incomplete Data*. Manual IV, New York, United Nations, 1967, pp. 17-21

26. K. Srinivasan, *Basic Demographic Techniques and Applications, op. cit*, p. 168

27. H. S. Shyrock, *et. al.* (*ed*), *Method and Materials of Demography, op. cit.* p. 123

28. Pakyntein, in *Census of India 1971*, Assam, General Report Series -3, Part 1-A, p. 10

29. The percentage is calculated from smoothened and unsmoothened population, as shown in *Census of India 1971. Age and Life Tables Paper* 2 of 1974, *op cit.* pp. 9-10

30. H. S. Shyrock, *et al* (ed), *Methods and Materials of Demography*, *op cit.*, p. 126

3

MORTALITY RATES AND LIFE TABLES

In Chapter II the age specific population data have been smoothened. In order to arrive at age specific population in a succeeding census from the age specific population of preceding census, the age specific survival ratios are required. To work out these ratios, decade-wise life tables are to be constructed. This chapter is devoted to this task of constructing life tables for Assam of the decades 1961-71, 1971-81 and 1981-91 and for the period 1971-91. Since age specific mortality rates of Assam for the decade 1951-61 are not available, the life table constructed by Kohli[1] for the decade 1951-61 is used to work out survival ratio for the decade. The life tables for the decades and the period mentioned above are constructed on the basis of age specific mortality rates provided by the SRS (Sample Registration System). According to Bhattacharjee, SRS is the only source which provides relatively more dependable data on fertility and mortality.[2] Bhende *et al.* also believe that the estimates of the SRS are fairly reliable.[3] The marked improvement of the SRS in the direction of level of results attained, is observed from the year 1968.[4] Therefore the SRS age specific mortality rates since 1968 are taken for constructing life tables.

The SRS Age Specific Mortality Rates (APMRs)

The SRS has been providing age specific death rates since 1965-67 for rural Assam.[5] Before 1965-67, there was an experimental study conducted by SRS on rural areas in 1964-65.[6] However, the APMR estimate furnished by the Report of 1965-67 is not at all satisfactory, because it gives such a crude death rate (15.7)[7] that is not at all close to the census crude death rate of 19.6 for Assam.[8] The next systematic sample survey was done by the SRS in 1968 for most of the states of India (rural) including Assam. The SRS age specific death rates of 1968 and 1969 can be considered satisfactory because crude death rates of 1968 (19.96) and 1969 (17.76) are close to that of the census crude (central) death rate (19.6) of Assam for the decade 1961-71. Therefore the age specific death rate of 1968 and 1969 are taken as decadal age specific death rate for the decade (1961-71) after making necessary adjustment.

The SRS has been providing year-wise age specific death rates since 1968. As the SRS total death rates since 1968 are close to the census total death rate, therefore, for constructing life table for the decades 1961-71, 1971-81, 1981-91 and 1981-91 the SRS age specific death rates are taken.

Rationale for Adjustment

The risk of death, in the most of the underdeveloped countries is very high in two extremes of life infancy and the old age. Conventionally the risk of death touches the lowest point in the age group 10-14 and after age 14 the risk of dying begins to rise gradually up to about mid forties. Thereafter the risk of death increases rapidly with age.[9] On the contrary, the risk during infancy and childhood in most of advanced countries is very small; it increases slowly with age.[10] Assam also experiences the former type of age specific mortality rates, being an underdeveloped state. However, it has been observed that the age specific mortality rates computed by the SRS are not smooth enough for constructing life table. The acceptability of a life table depends on the systematic arrangement of APMRS. If APMRs are not systematically arranged then the 'values of life table functions' will be unsystematically arranged. For instance the most important outcome of life table is expectations of life at various ages of life. The expectations of life decrease with the age. If there is an abrupt fluctuation or zigzag in APMRs then the expectations of life at various ages and other functions of the life table will show fluctuations, defeating the very purpose of life table.

Therefore the age specific mortality rates provided by the SRS have to be adjusted and smoothened as and when necessary. Moreover, the SRS has provided APMRs up to the age group 65-69. But for our purpose APMRs up to age 90+ are required. Therefore age specific mortality rates beyond the age group 65-69 are to be extrapolated. The procedures of adjustment, smoothening and extrapolation of APMRs are given below.

Decade 1961-71

1. Average age specific mortality rates of 1968 and 1969 (rural Assam) are considered to be best fit for the decade 1961-71, as the total death rates are close to the census decadal total (central) death rate. However, it has been found that the average of the death rates of 1968 and 1969 (18.66) is marginally lower than that of the census total death rate of 19.6. Therefore all the age specific death rates (average of 1968 and 1969) are adjusted with the census central death rate for both male and female.

2. The age specific mortality rates are found to be highly fluctuating specially in the age groups from 20-24 to 35-40. The fluctuations in the age specific mortality rates are smoothened part by part by fitting regression equation in those particular age groups.

3. The regression equation and the age specific mortality rates (in original and smoothened for both male and female for the decade 1961-71) are as follows

(a) Age specific mortality rates for selected age groups (Male) : Original and smoothened

Age group	*APMR Original*	*APMR Smoothed*
20-24	4.17	3.74
25-29	3.71	4.57
30-34	5.84	5.41

Regression equation : Y= 4.57 + .835X

(b) Age specific mortality rates for selected age groups (Female) : Original and smoothened

Age group	*APMR Original*	*APMR Smoothed*
20-24	7.57	6.57
25-29	10.79	8.89
30-34	11.47	11.21
35-39	10.75	13.54
40-44	14.31	15.86
45-49	13.27	18.19
50-54	26.65	20.51

Regression equation : Y = 13.543 + 2.3228X

4. The Mortality Rates Beyond Age group 65-69

The age specific mortality rates in the age groups beyond 65-69 are generally derived by extrapolating the observed trends in the mortality rates age groups adjacent to the last. It is found that the values of original age specific mortality rates of age groups from 55-59 to 65-69 or 50-54 to 65-69 are well fitted to have an equation for extrapolating mortality rates. . Kohli[11] and . Jain[12] have applied the least square method for projecting age specific mortality rates (survival ratios) in constructing life tables for all the states of India for the decade. 1951-61 and life table for India for the decade 1951-61 respectively. Therefore, the APMRs beyond age group 65-69 are extrapolated by fitting regression equations which are as follows

(a)Regression equations based on APMRs of age groups 55-59 to 65-69

$$Y = 55.46 + 22.74X \text{ (male)}$$
$$Y = 48.04 + 33.885X - 17.40X^2 \text{ (female)}$$

The third degree regression equation is best fitted for female.

(b)Regression equations based on APMRs of age groups 50-54 to 65-69.

$$Y = 48.085 + 8.966X \text{ (male)}$$
$$Y = 51.395 + 11.726X \text{ (female)}$$

5. Female age specific Mortality Rates in the Age group 0-4

It has found that female APMR in age group 0-4 in 1968 is 53.36, which drops appreciably to 39.8 in 1969. It is to be noted that female APMRs for Assam in age group 0-4 in 1970, 1972, and 1974 are found to be 44.4, 58.5 and 50.3 respectively.[13] The average male APMR in age group 0-4 for the years 1968 and 1969 is 53.23. Therefore female APMR suddenly dropping to 39.8 in 1969 is doubtful. Observing the trend of female APMRs and taking into account male APMR in age 0-4, the female APMR of 1968 of 53.36 appears more authentic. Hence this rate is taken.

6. The original, (average age specific mortality rates of the years 1968 and 1969) adjusted and smoothened age specific mortality rates for the decade 1961-71 are given in Table 3.1 (the total APMRs are estimated by averaging the male and female mortality rates).

Decade 1971 – 81

1. The average APMRs for this decade (1971-81) are worked out from the SRS estimates of APMRs for the years 1971, 1976 and 1981.[14] The fluctuations in the average APMRs are smoothened by applying the least square method.

Table 3.1 : Original Average, Adjusted and Smoothened Age Specific Mortality rates for the decades 1961-71

Age group	*1961-71 Average*			*Age group*	*1961-71 Adjusted*			*1961-71 Smoothed*		
	Total	*Male*	*Female*		*Total*	*Male*	*Female*	*Total*	*Male*	*Female*
0 to 4	53.30	53.23	53.36	0 to 4	55.98	55.91	56.04	55.98	55.91	56.04
5 to 9	6.40	6.34	6.46	5 to 9	6.73	6.66	6.79	6.73	6.66	6.79
10 to 14	3.45	3.05	3.84	10 to 14	3.62	3.20	4.03	3.62	3.20	4.03
15 to 19	3.34	2.46	4.22	15 to 19	3.51	2.58	4.43	3.51	2.58	4.43
20 to 24	5.59	3.97	7.21	20 to 24	5.87	4.17	7.57	5.16	3.74	6.57
25 to 29	6.91	3.54	10.27	25 to 29	7.25	3.71	10.79	6.73	4.57	8.89
30 to 34	8.24	5.56	10.92	30 to 34	8.66	5.84	11.47	8.31	5.41	11.21
35 to 39	8.73	7.22	10.23	35 to 39	9.17	7.58	10.75	10.20	6.85	13.54
40 to 44	10.93	8.23	13.62	40 to 44	11.48	8.64	14.31	14.55	13.23	15.86
45 to 49	18.38	24.12	12.63	45 to 49	19.31	25.34	13.27	18.90	19.61	18.19
50 to 54	24.75	24.13	25.37	50 to 54	26.00	25.34	26.65	23.25	25.99	20.51
55 to 59	29.85	29.64	30.05	55 to 59	31.35	31.13	31.56	31.97	32.37	31.56
60 to 64	49.60	53.45	45.74	60 to 64	52.09	56.14	48.04	52.09	56.14	48.04
65 to 69	84.34	74.11	94.57	65 to 69	88.59	77.84	99.33	71.19	77.84	64.53
70 +	132.62	130.00	135.24	70 to 74				86.98	92.92	81.04
All ages	18.67	18.68	18.65	*				105.48	100.94	110.02
				75 to 79				104.17	110.84	97.50
				*				128.56	123.64	133.48
				80 to 84				121.38	128.78	113.98
				*				151.68	146.42	156.93
				85 to 89				138.59	146.71	130.46
				*				174.77	169.16	180.38
				90 +				155.80	164.64	146.95
				*				197.87	191.90	203.83

*Indicates the mortality rates estimated by using of regression equation based on APMRs of last three age groups.

Source : *Measures of Fertility and Mortality in India*, 1968-1969, SRS Analytical Series No. 2, 1972

Table 3.2 : Original Average Age Specific Mortality Rates for the decades 1971-81 and 1981-91 and for the period 1971-91

Age group	1971-81			1981-91			1971-91		
	Total	Male	Female	Total	Male	Female	Total	Male	Female
0 to 4	40.40	40.68	40.06	43.07	43.10	42.90	37.43	36.93	37.97
5 to 9	5.44	4.94	5.98	5.83	5.53	6.13	4.63	3.83	5.50
10 to 14	2.80	2.56	3.02	3.07	2.80	3.30	2.60	2.53	2.67
15 to 19	2.78	2.10	3.46	2.83	1.93	3.73	2.60	2.30	2.90
20 to 24	4.26	3.02	5.38	4.43	3.20	5.57	4.00	2.97	4.93
25 to 29	5.20	3.42	7.00	5.80	3.83	7.78	4.63	3.63	5.63
30 to 34	6.52	4.36	8.84	7.37	4.17	10.77	6.00	4.37	7.77
35 to 39	5.82	5.68	5.98	6.13	6.00	6.30	5.10	4.63	5.63
40 to 44	9.74	10.68	8.62	1.13	12.70	9.26	7.97	7.67	8.37
45 to 49	13.06	15.06	10.46	15.33	17.26	12.70	10.00	11.27	8.43
50 to 54	21.02	21.98	19.78	22.83	23.23	22.23	20.27	23.07	16.63
55 to 59	26.76	30.38	21.98	28.47	33.86	21.30	24.47	27.00	21.27
60 to 64	43.88	44.54	43.10	46.83	46.63	47.17	41.10	42.17	39.77
65 to 69	70.32	74.66	64.68	76.23	79.53	71.93	62.50	65.70	58.23
70 +	109.76	111.48	107.36	114.00	117.17	109.67	100.57	104.30	95.13
All ages	13.88	14.10	13.58	15.10	15.40	14.70	12.23	12.27	12.17

Derived from *Compendium of India's Fertility and Mortality Indicators*, 1971-1997 based on the SRS RG India, 1999

Table 3.3 : Smoothened Age Specific Mortality Rates for the decades 1971-81 and 1981-91 and for the period 1971-91

Age group	*1971-91*			*1971-81*			*1981-91*		
	Total	*Male*	*Female*	*Total*	*Male*	*Female*	*Total*	*Male*	*Female*
0 to 4	40.40	40.68	40.06	43.07	43.10	42.90	37.43	36.93	37.97
5 to 9	5.44	4.94	5.98	5.83	5.53	6.13	4.63	3.83	5.50
10 to 14	2.80	25.60	3.02	3.07	2.80	3.30	2.60	2.53	2.67
15 to 19	2.78	2.10	3.46	2.83	1.93	3.73	2.60	2.30	2.90
20 to 24	4.26	3.02	5.38	4.43	3.20	5.57	40.00	2.97	4.93
25 to 29	5.26	3.42	7.00	5.80	3.83	7.78	4.63	3.63	5.63
30 to 34	5.75	3.75	7.35	6.33	4.17	8.45	5.37	4.37	6.89
35 to 39	7.36	6.91	8.10	8.21	7.62	9.32	6.35	4.63	7.31
40 to 44	8.97	10.06	8.45	10.90	12.70	10.20	7.34	7.67	7.79
45 to 49	13.06	15.06	9.60	15.33	17.26	11.07	10.00	11.27	8.26
50 to 54	21.02	21.98	19.78	22.83	23.23	22.23	20.27	23.07	16.63
55 to 59	26.76	30.38	21.98	28.47	33.86	23.70	24.47	27.00	21.27
60 to 64	43.88	44.54	43.10	46.83	46.63	47.17	41.10	42.17	39.77
65 to 69	70.32	74.66	64.68	76.23	79.53	71.93	62.50	65.70	58.23
70 to 74	81.75	85.94	76.33	87.57	91.21	84.39	73.08	75.25	69.80
*	90.58	94.14	85.95	98.27	99.01	95.83	80.72	83.66	76.72
75 to 79	98.25	103.16	91.92	105.43	109.37	101.65	87.44	89.56	84.13
*	112.36	116.36	107.30	122.15	121.85	119.95	99.74	103.01	95.20
80 to 84	114.75	120.38	107.50	123.29	127.53	118.91	101.80	103.86	98.46
*	134.14	138.42	128.65	146.03	144.68	114.06	118.75	122.36	113.70
85 to 89	131.24	137.60	123.08	141.15	145.69	136.16	116.16	118.17	112.79
*	155.92	160.56	150.00	169.91	167.52	168.18	137.76	141.71	132.16
90 +	147.75	154.82	138.66	159.01	163.85	153.42	130.52	132.47	127.12
*	177.70	182.70	171.35	193.79	190.35	192.29	156.78	161.06	150.64

***Indicates the mortality rates estimated by using of regression equation based on APMRs of last three age groups.**

Derived from Table 3.2

2. The male APMRs as provided by the SRS are found to be smooth. Hence the original values have been retained without any alternation. The smoothened APMRs of total and female for age groups from 30-34 to 40-44 and 30-34 to 45-49 respectively and their corresponding regression equations (based on original APMRs) are as follows :

(a) Age specific mortality rates for selected age groups : (female and total) original and smoothened

Age Group	Total APMR		Female APMR	
	Original	Smoothened	Original	Smoothened
30-34	7.37	6.33	10.77	8.45
35-39	6.13	8.21	6.30	9.32
40-44	11.13	10.09	9.26	10.20
45-49	-	-	12.70	11.07

Regression equations –

Total – $Y = 8.21 + 1.88X$

Female - $Y = 9.7575 + .4375X$

3. Regression equations for age groups 70-74 to 90+.

(a) Based on last three age groups' APMRs

Total $Y = 50.51 + 23.88X$

Male $Y = 53.34 + 22.835X$

Female $Y = 47.6 + 24.115X$

(b) Based on last four age groups' APMRs

Total $Y = 42.92 + 8.93X$

Male $Y = 45.81 + 9.08X$

Female $Y = 41.25 + 8.629X$

Decade 1981-91

1. The average APMRs for decade 1981-91 are worked out from the SRS estimates of APMRs for years 1981, 1986 and 1991.[15] The fluctuations in the average age specific mortality rates for the decade are smoothened by applying the least square method.

2. The original male APMRs are retained because these are found to be smooth. The smoothened APMRs of total and female for the age groups 30-34 to 40-44 and 30-34 to 45-49 respectively and their corresponding regression equations (based on original APMRs) are as follows.

(a) Age specific mortality rates for specific age groups (total and female) : Original and smoothened

Age Group	Total APMR		Female APMR	
	Original	Smoothened	Original	Smoothened
30-34	6.0	5.37	7.77	6.89
35-39	5.1	6.35	5.63	7.31
40-44	7.97	7.34	8.37	7.79
45-49	-	-	8.84	8.26

Regression equations –

Total Y = 6.35 + .985X
Female Y = 7.55 + .236X

(b)Regression equations for the age groups 70-74 to 90+

(i) Based on last three age groups' APMRs

Total Y = 42.69 + 19.015X
Male Y = 44.956 + 19.35X
Female Y = 39.756 + 18.48X

(ii) Based on last four age groups' APMRs

Total Y = 37.18 + 7.18X
Male Y = 39.485 + 7.153X
Female Y = 33.975 + 7.165X

Period 1971-91

In Assam there was no census operation in 1981. Consequently we do not find distribution of population by quinquennial age group for the decade 1971-81. Therefore a life table for period 1971-91 is required to be constructed for projecting 1971 population to 1991. However, the life tables for decades 1971-81 and 1981-91 are also required to be constructed to workout survival ratios and survivors in the age-groups 0-4, 5-9, 10-14 and 15-19 for the Census year 1991, as the survival ratio of 1971-91 life table cannot provide the basis for population projection in the age groups below 20-24.

1. The average APMRs for period 1971-91 are estimated from the SRS age specific mortality rates of years 1971, 1976, 1981, 1986, and 1991. The fluctuations in the average APMRs are smoothened by applying the least square method, where found necessary.

2. The smoothened APMRs for male, female, and total for the age groups from 30-34 to 40-44 (for male and total) and 30-34 to 40-44 (for

female) and their regression equations (based on original APMRs) are as follows for the period 1971-91.

(a) Age specific mortality rates for selected age group : original and total

Age group	*Total APMR*		*Male APMR*		*Female APMR*	
	Original	*Smoothened*	*Original*	*Smoothened*	*Original*	*Smoothened*
30-34	6.52	5.75	4.36	3.75	8.84	7.35
35-39	5.82	7.36	5.68	6.91	5.98	8.10
40-44	9.74	8.97	10.68	10.06	8.62	8.45
45-49	-	-	-	-	10.46	9.60

Regression equations

Total Y = 7.36 + 1.61X
Male Y = 6.905 + 3.16X
Female Y = 7.5 + .375X

3. Regression equations for the age groups from 70-74 to 90+

(a) Based on last three age groups' APMRs

Total Y = 47.02 + 21.78X
Male Y = 49.86 + 22.14X
Female Y = 43.25 + 21.35X

(b) Based on last four age groups' APMRs

Total Y = 40.495 + 8.25X
Male Y = 45.81 + 9.08X
Female Y = 37.385 + 7.79X

The original average APMRs and smoothened APMS for the age group 0-4 to 70 + and 0-4 to 90 + are given in Tables 3.2 and 3.3 respectively for the decades 1971-81 and 1981-91 and for the period 1971-91.

Estimating Sex Specific Infant and Child (1-4 age group) Mortality Rates

In the SRS reports sex specific infant and 1-4 age group (for all the years) mortality rates (for the decades 1961-71 and 1971-81) are not available, (only infant mortality rates by rural and urban areas and 0-4 age group mortality rates by sex and areas are available). To construct life table, sex specific infant and 4 year mortality rates are required. These are estimated as follows :

The ratios of sex specific infant mortality rates for the decade 1951-61 and for the period 1982-1991 are estimated and applied to find out sex specific infant mortality for the decade 1961-71 and 1971-81 respectively, assuming that ratios of male and female infant mortality rates of the preceding decade remained unattached in the succeeding decade. Noteworthy that Sex specific infant mortality rates for decade 1951-61 (as worked out by K.L. Kohli[16]) and for the years 1982 to 1991, (as provided by SRS) are available.

Estimating 1-4 age group mortality rate

To estimate 1-4 age group mortality rate, total population and number of deaths in the age

group 1-4 are required. The estimating procedure of the above is as follows :

Method – 1

(a) 1-4 age group population can be estimated as the difference between the total number of births (i.e. the product of mid census year population and official decadal birth rate) and total number of infant deaths (i.e. the product of births and IMR) of a decade;

(b) 1-4 age group deaths can be estimated as the difference between 0-4 age group total deaths (i.e. the product of total number of birth and 0-4 age group mortality rate) and total infant deaths (i.e. the product of births and IMR); and

(c) 1-4 age group mortality rate is a ratio per 1000 population between 1-4 age group deaths and population.

Method – 2

(a) In constructing life tables mortality rates are to be converted into q_x values (i.e. probability of dying in between two specified age groups). If q_x value of any age group can be derived from the relations of 'life-table-functions' then there is no need of estimating mortality rates in that particular age or age group. As the SRS has provided '0-4' and '0' age groups mortality rates (m_x), the q_x values of '0-4' and '0' age groups can be derived. Hence there is no need of estimating 1-4 age group mortality rate. This (i.e. q_x of 1-4 age group) can be directly worked out from the values of l_x, d_x and q_x of the life table.

The relation between l_x, d_x and q_x in a life table is as follows :

$d_x = q_x \cdot l_x$ or $q_x = d_x / l_x$

These relations imply that if d_x and l_x in a particular age group can be derived then q_x can be directly worked out. The d_x of 1-4 age group will be equal to the difference between 0-4 age group d_x and '0' age d_x, and l_x of 1-4 age group will be equal to the difference between l_x of '0' age and d_x of '0' age. For instance if l_0 = 1,00,000, q_0 = .13032 and q_{0-4} = .24540, then q_{1-4} will be as shown in Table 3.4.

Table 3.4 : 1-4 age group q_x, l_x and d_x

Age	q_x	l_x	d_x
0 – 4	.24540	1,00,000	24540
0	.13032	1,00,000	13032
1 - 4	.11085	84668	9408

Table 3.10 shows that d_x of 1-4 age group is the difference between the age group 0-4 and age 0 and similarly l_x is a difference between the l_x of '0' age and dx of 0 age. Finally q_x in the age group 1-4 is direct result of d_x / l_x the age group 1-4.

Out of two methods, the latter one is selected for estimating 1-4 age group qx value, as this method directly gives the qx value.

The smoothened and adjusted age specific mortality rates from age group 0 onward are used to construct life table for decades 1961-71, 1971-81, 1981-91 and 1971-91, so as to find out the 10 year and 20 year survival ratios.

Construction of Life Table

"The life table is life history of a hypothetical group or cohort of people, as it is diminished gradually by deaths".[17] Generally life tables are of two types; complete and abridged, a complete life table contains data for every single year age, whereas an abridged life table contains data by certain age intervals. It has been recommended that the values of 5 or 10 years' intervals are sufficiently accurate for most purposes and an abridged life table is less burdensome to prepare.[18] As mortality rates of quinquennial age group are only available, therefore it is necessary to construct 5-year age interval abridged life table.

The Anatomy of Life Table

The basic functions of life table are –

${}_nq_x$, l_x, ${}_nd_x$, ${}_nL_x$, T_x and $\mathring{e}_x$. These functions can be explained as –

1. **n** is the age interval from one exact age(x) to another age (x+n).

2. $_nq_x$ is the probability of dying between the age x and x+n. [19]

3. l_x is the number of survivors in the exact age x. The l_x is initially assumed as 1,00,000 live births, at the age '0'. This number 1,00,000 is assumed again as radix or initial cohort of the life table.

4. $_nd_x$ is the number of death between exact age x and x + n out of the total number of births assumed in the life table.

5. $_nl_x$ is the number of years lived during the interval year x and x + n by the cohort of 1,00,000.

6. T_x is the person-years lived after attaining exact age x till death.

7. $\ddot{e}_x$ is the expectation of average life at any given age.

Interrelation between the Life Table Functions

(a) Age specific or single year $_nq_x$ values constitute the core of a life table. Then $_nq_x$ are derived from age specific mortality rates. The methods commonly used to convert age specific mortality rates ($_n\mathbf{M}_x$) into probability at age x of dying ($_nq_x$) are as follows –

1. The Reed Merrell method
2. T.N.E. Gravelle's method and
3. Standard Life Table method.

The procedures of transforming **nMx** into $_nq_x$ by each of these three methods are given below.[20]

1. The Reed-Merrell method

$$_n\mathbf{q}_x = \mathbf{1\text{-}e}^{-n} \cdot {}_n\mathbf{m}_x - \mathbf{an}^3 \cdot {}_n\mathbf{m}_x^{\ 2}$$

$$_n\mathbf{q}_x = \mathbf{1\text{-}e}$$

Where **n** is the size of the age interval, $_n\mathbf{m}_x$ is central (age specific) death rate, **a** is a constant, and **e** is the base of natural logithims system.

2. Greville's methods

$$_nq_x = \frac{_n\mathbf{m}_x}{1/n + {}_n\mathbf{m}_x \ \{1/2 - \mathbf{n/12}({}_n\mathbf{m}_x - \mathbf{Log.\ e})\}}$$

Where **n** is the size of age interval, $_n\mathbf{m}_x$ is the age specific mortality rate and log **e** is equal to .095.

3. Standard Life Table method

$$ {}_nq_x = \frac{{}_nm_x}{1 + {}_ng_x \cdot {}_nm_x} $$

The value ${}_ng_x$ is computed for the standard life table on the basis of the observed central death rate (${}_nm_x$) and the mortality rate (${}_nq_x$) using the formula[21]-

$$ {}_nq_x = \frac{n}{{}_nq_x} - \frac{1}{{}_nm_x} $$

It has been observed that the values of ${}_nq_x$, completed from ${}_nm_x$, by all these three methods are close to one another.[22] Both the Reed-Merrell and Grevelle's methods give similar expectation of life at different age groups. For instance, expectations of life at birth computed by following the Reed-Merrell and Grevelle's method, from the N.S.S.O.'s (National Sample Survey Organization) ${}_nl_x$ of India (rural males) for 1957-58 are 43.71 and 43.95 respectively. This indicates that any of the methods holds good for making estimate.

In our study ${}_nm_x$ are converted into ${}_nq_x$ by applying Greville's method.

(b) lo (number of Survivors to the exact age 0 or x) is assumed to be 1,00,000.

$$ lx = 1,00,000 $$
$$ l_{x+1} = l_x - {}_nd_x $$

(c) ${}_nd_x$ (number of death between exact age x and x+1) is inter related as -

$$ {}_nd_x = l_x \cdot {}_nq_x $$

(d) ${}_nL_x$ (number of person years lived within the interval year **x** and **x+n**) is interrelated as -

$$ Lo = .276\, lo + .724\, l_x $$
$$ 4L_1 = .034\, lo + .1.184\, l_1 + 2.782\, l_2 $$

For the age group beyond 1-4 the relationships used are –

$$ {}_nL_x = n/2(l_x + l_{x+n}) + n/24\, ({}_nd_{x+n} - {}_nd_{x-n}) $$
or simply,
$$ {}_nL_x = n/2\, (l_x + l_{x+n}) $$

Both the relations of ${}_{n}\mathbf{L}_{x}$ shown above give similar survival ratios and both are used separately.

$${}_{w}\mathbf{L}_{x} = {}_{n}\mathbf{d}_{x} \ / \ {}_{w}\mathbf{m}_{x}$$

Where w is the terminal age group and ${}_{n}\mathbf{m}_{x}$ is the mortality rate of last age group.

(e) ${}_{n}\mathbf{T}_{x}$ (person year lived) is related as

$${}_{w}\mathbf{T}_{x} = {}_{w}\mathbf{L}_{x}$$

Where w is the terminal or last age group.

$${}_{n}\mathbf{T}_{x} = {}_{n}\mathbf{L}_{x} + {}_{n}\mathbf{L}_{x-n}$$

${}_{n}\mathbf{T}_{x}$ is computed from last age group onwards.

(f) $\ddot{e}_{x}$ (expectation of life at various age group) is related as –

$$\ddot{e}_{x} = {}_{n}\mathbf{T}_{x} \ / \ \mathbf{L}_{x}$$

Survival Ratios

"Survival rates are defined in terms of two ages, and hence two time references, the initial age and date and the terminal age and date ..... Survival rates express survival from younger age to older age".[23]

The most common form of survival rate that is computed for a 5-year age group and a 10-year time period is –

$${}_{5}\mathbf{S}_{x}^{10} = {}_{5}\mathbf{L}_{x} + 10 \ / \ {}_{5}\mathbf{L}_{x}$$

Where ${}_{5}\mathbf{S}_{x}^{10}$ is the survival rate of 5-year age group population rate age x for 10-year time period and ${}_{5}\mathbf{L}_{x+10}$ and ${}_{5}\mathbf{L}_{x}$ are the values of 'persons years lived' at the age groups x+10 and x respectively. This indicates the probability of a person or group of persons surviving for another 10 years. From the life tables computed by applying the method mentioned above the survival rates are also worked out.

The life tables constructed (Sets 1 and 2) by following the procedure mentioned above are presented by Tables 3.5 to 3.28. The life tables for the decade 1951-1961 (Tables 3.29 and 3.30) are constructed by Kohli.

It may be noted that both sets of life table yield similar expectation of life at birth and hence either set may be used. We have however used the life table where the APMRs of age groups above 65-69 are projected by applying regression equation estimated on the basis of last three age groups' APMRs. And it may again be mentioned that, out of two sets of survival ratios of a deca lal life table either sets of survival ratio may be used because both yield more or less similar results.

References

1. K.L. Kohli : *Mortality in India, op. cit*, pp 228-231.

2. B.N. Bhattacharjee : "Some Aspect of Mortality Statistics in India" in Bose A., *et al. (ed)* : *Population Statistics in India*, Vikas Publishing House Pvt. Ltd., New Delhi, 1977, p. 251.

3. A.A. Ghende, and T. Kanitkar : *Principles of Population Studies*, Himalaya Publishing House, 1978, p. 55.

4. A. Mitra : *India's Population*, Abhinav Publications, New Delhi, 1978, p. 84.

5. Sample Registration in India : Report on Rural Areas 1965-67, Registrar General India.

6. *ibid*, p.6.

7. *ibid*, p. IX.

8. *Census of India*, Series I- India Paper 1 of 1977. Life Tables. Registrar General and Census Commissioner, India, p. 38.

9. K.L. Kohli : *Mortality in India, op cit.* p. 85.

10. H.S. Shryock, et. al. : *Methods and Materials of Demography, op. cit*, p. 227.

11. K.L. Kohli : *Mortality in India, op. cit*, p. 47.

12. S.P. Jain : *Census of India*, 1961, Paper 2 of 1963, Life Tables 1951-61, p. 18.

13. *Report on SRS in Eastern Zone*, 1970-75, R.G. India, Vital Statistics Division, New Delhi, 1981, p. 29.

14. *Compendium of India's Fertility and Mortality Indicators 1971-91*, based on the SRS. R.G. India, 1999, p. 46.

15. *Compendium of India's Fertility and Mortality, op. cit*, p. 46.

16. K.L. Kohli : *Mortality in India*, op. cit., pp. 228-229

17. G.W. Barclay : *Technique of Population Analysis*, John Willey & Sons, New York 1958, p. 93.

18. H.S. Shryock, *et al* : *Methods and Materials of Demography, op. cit*, 1976, p. 249

19. *ibid*, p. 251.

20. *ibid*, pp. 254-256.

21. *ibid*, p. 256.

22. *ibid*, p. 257.

23. *ibid*, p. 262.

Table : 3.5 Male Abridged Life table : Assam : 1961-71 (Set – 1)

Age	*Mx*	*Qx*	*lx*	*dx*	*Lx*	*Lx1*	*Tx*	*ex*	*SR*	*SR1*
0-4	0.05591	0.24625	100000	24625	402620	402620	4388410			
0-	0.15132	0.15132	100000	15132	89044	89044	4388410	43.88		
1 to 4		0.11186	84868	9493	313576	313576	4299365	50.66		
5 to 9	0.00666	0.03279	75375	2472	370694	370371	3985789	52.88		
10 to 14	0.00321	0.01593	72903	1161	361610	361642	3615418	49.59	0.89814	0.89822
15 to 19	0.00258	0.01282	71741	921	356404	356540	3253777	45.35	0.96145	0.96266
20 to 24	0.00374	0.01854	70820	1313	350819	350924	2897237	40.91	0.97016	0.97036
25 to 29	0.00457	0.02261	69507	1572	343608	343745	2546313	36.63	0.96410	0.96411
30 to 34	0.00541	0.02672	67936	1815	335141	335617	2202569	32.42	0.95531	0.95638
35 to 39	0.00685	0.03372	66121	2229	325031	325734	1866951	28.24	0.94594	0.94760
40 to 44	0.01323	0.06417	63891	4100	309207	309735	1541217	24.12	0.92262	0.92288
45 to 49	0.01961	0.09374	59791	5605	284945	285266	1231482	20.60	0.87667	0.87576
50 to 54	0.02599	0.12245	54186	6635	254344	255042	946216	17.46	0.82257	0.82342
55 to 59	0.03237	0.15032	47551	7148	219886	220467	691174	14.54	0.77168	0.77285
60 to 64	0.05614	0.24714	40403	9985	177054	176692	470707	11.65	0.69612	0.69279
65 to 69	0.07784	0.32656	30418	9933	127257	126385	294016	9.67	0.57874	0.57326
70 to 74	0.10094	0.40260	20485	8247	81806	80804	167631	8.18	0.46204	0.45732
75 to 79	0.12364	0.46959	12238	5747	46821	45995	86827	7.10	0.36793	0.36393
80 to 84	0.14642	0.52984	6491	3439	23857	23405	40831	6.29	0.29163	0.28965
85 to 89	0.16916	0.58370	3052	1781	10806	10806	17426	5.71	0.23078	0.23493
90 +	0.19190	0.63188	1270	1270	6620	6620	6620	5.21	0.27751	0.28286

Table 3.6: Female Abridged Life table : Assam : 1961-71 (Set – 1)

Age	*Mx*	*qx*	*lx*	*dx*	*Lx*	*Lx1*	*Tx*	*ex*	*SR*	*SR1*
0-4	0.05604	0.24675	100000	24675	404514	404514	4170808			
0-	0.14068	0.14068	100000	14068	89815	89815	4170808	41.71		
1 to 4		0.12343	85932	10607	314699	314699	4080993	47.49		
5 to 9	0.00679	0.03342	75325	2518	370333	370000	3766295	50.00		
10 to 14	0.00403	0.01996	72808	1454	360405	360577	3396294	46.65	0.89096	0.89138
15 to 19	0.00443	0.02193	71354	921	354468	354895	3035718	42.54	0.95716	0.95917
20 to 24	0.00657	0.03236	70433	2279	346468	346735	2680823	38.06	0.96133	0.96161
25 to 29	0.00889	0.04355	68154	2968	333350	333574	2334088	34.25	0.94042	0.93992
30 to 34	0.01121	0.05463	65186	3561	317027	317203	2000513	30.69	0.91503	0.91483
35 to 39	0.01354	0.06563	61625	4044	298014	298138	1683310	27.32	0.89400	0.89377
40 to 44	0.01586	0.07647	57581	4403	276896	276968	1385172	24.06	0.87341	0.87316
45 to 49	0.01819	0.08724	53178	4639	254290	254663	1108205	20.84	0.85328	0.85418
50 to 54	0.02051	0.09784	48539	4749	230820	231506	853541	17.58	0.83360	0.83586
55 to 59	0.03156	0.14683	43789	6429	202873	203961	622035	14.21	0.79780	0.80091
60 to 64	0.04804	0.21535	37360	8045	166686	166593	418074	11.19	0.72215	0.71960
65 to 69	0.09933	0.39757	29314	11654	117436	116049	251481	8.58	0.57887	0.56897
70 to 74	0.11002	0.43027	17660	7599	69303	68307	135433	7.67	0.41577	0.41002
75 to 79	0.13348	0.49643	10061	4995	37820	37065	67126	6.67	0.32205	0.31939
80 to 84	0.15693	0.55548	5067	2814	18297	17895	30061	5.93	0.26401	0.26198
85 to 89	0.18038	0.60814	2252	1370	7837	7837	12167	5.40	0.20722	0.21144
90 +	0.20383	0.65507	883	883	4330	4330	4330	4.91	0.23664	0.24196

Table 3.7 : Total (Male and Female) Abridged Life table : Assam : 1961-71 (Set – 1)

Age	*Mx*	*qx*	*lx*	*dx*	*Lx*	*Lx1*	*Tx*	*ex*	*SR*	*SR1*
0-4	0.05598	0.24652	100000	24652	403563	403563	4295246			
0-	0.14600	0.14600	100000	14600	89430	89430	4295246	42.95		
1 to 4		0.11770	85400	10052	314133	314133	4205817	49.25		
5 to 9	0.00673	0.03313	75348	2497	370501	370172	3891684	51.65		
10 to 14	0.00362	0.01795	72852	1308	360990	361093	3521511	48.34	0.89451	
0.89476	15 to 19	0.00351	0.01741	71544	921	355418	355702	3160419	44.17	
0.95929	0.96091	20 to 24	0.00516	0.02550	70623	1801	348614	348804	2804717	39.71
0.96572	0.96597	25 to 29	0.00673	0.03313	68823	2280	338412	338600	2455913	35.68
0.95215	0.95192	30 to 34	0.00831	0.04076	66542	2713	325930	326254	2117313	31.82
0.93493	0.93535	35 to 39	0.01020	0.04982	63830	3180	311199	311599	1791059	28.06
0.91958	0.92026	40 to 44	0.01455	0.07036	60650	4267	292580	292869	1479460	24.39
0.89768	0.89767	45 to 49	0.01890	0.09050	56382	5102	269156	269505	1186591	21.05
0.86490	0.86491	50 to 54	0.02325	0.11023	51280	5652	242269	242964	917086	17.88
0.82804	0.82960	55 to 59	0.03197	0.14860	45628	6780	211188	211660	674122	14.77
0.78463	0.78537	60 to 64	0.05209	0.23139	38847	8989	171765	171698	462462	11.90
0.70898	0.70668	65 to 69	0.07119	0.30308	29858	9049	126668	126005	290764	9.74
0.59979	0.59532	70 to 74	0.10548	0.41659	20809	8669	82373	81276	164759	7.92
0.47957	0.47337	75 to 79	0.12856	0.48317	12140	5866	46037	45171	83483	6.88
0.36344	0.35848	80 to 84	0.15168	0.54283	6274	3406	22857	22389	38312	6.11
0.27749	0.27547	85 to 89	0.17477	0.59609	2868	1710	10068	10068	15923	5.55
0.21869	0.22288	90 +	0.19787	0.64366	1159	1159	5855	5855	5855	5.05
0.25617	0.26153									

Table 3.8 : Male Abridged Life table : Assam : 1961-71 (Set – 2)

Age	*Mx*	*qx*	*lx*	*dx*	*Lx*	*Lx1*	*Tx*	*ex*	*SR*	*SR1*
0-4	0.05591	0.24625	100000	24625	402859	402859	4408396			
0-	0.15132	0.15132	100000	15132	89044	89044	4408396	44.08		
1 to 4		0.11085	84868	9408	313814	313814	4319351	50.89		
5 to 9	0.00666	0.03279	75460	2475	371115	370792	4005537	53.08		
10 to 14	0.00321	0.01593	72986	1163	362022	362053	3634745	49.80	0.89863	0.89871
15 to 19	0.00258	0.01282	71823	921	356812	356948	3272692	45.57	0.96146	0.96266
20 to 24	0.00374	0.01854	70902	1315	351223	351328	2915744	41.12	0.97017	0.97038
25 to 29	0.00457	0.02261	69587	1573	344003	344141	2564416	36.85	0.96410	0.96412
30 to 34	0.00541	0.02672	68014	1817	335527	336004	2220275	32.64	0.95531	0.95638
35 to 39	0.00685	0.03372	66197	2232	325405	326109	1884271	28.46	0.94594	0.94760
40 to 44	0.01323	0.06417	63965	4105	309564	310092	1558162	24.36	0.92262	0.92288
45 to 49	0.01961	0.09374	59860	5611	285273	285595	1248070	20.85	0.87667	0.87576
50 to 54	0.02599	0.12245	54249	6643	254637	255336	962475	17.74	0.82257	0.82342
55 to 59	0.03237	0.15032	47606	7156	220140	220721	707140	14.85	0.77168	0.77285
60 to 64	0.05614	0.24714	40450	9997	177258	176786	486419	12.03	0.69612	0.69237
65 to 69	0.07784	0.32656	30453	9945	127404	126484	309633	10.17	0.57874	0.57305
70 to 74	0.09292	0.37714	20508	7735	83205	82324	183149	8.93	0.46940	0.46567
75 to 79	0.11084	0.43271	12774	5527	50051	49313	100825	7.89	0.39285	0.38987
80 to 84	0.12878	0.48377	7246	3506	27468	27104	51512	7.11	0.33012	0.32923
85 to 89	0.14671	0.53057	3741	1985	13742	13742	24408	6.52	0.27457	0.27868
90 +	0.16464	0.57346	1756	1756	10666	10666	10666	6.07	0.38831	0.39353

Table 3.9 : Female Abridged Life table : Assam : 1961-71 (Set – 2)

Age	*Mx*	*qx*	*Lx*	*Dx*	*Lx*	*Lx1*	*Tx*	*ex*	*SR*	*SR1*
0-4	0.05604	0.24675	100000	24675	413426	413426	4382938			
0-	0.14068	0.14068	100000	14068	89815	89815	4382938	43.83		
1 to 4		0.08615	85932	7403	323611	323611	4293124	49.96		
5 to 9	0.00679	0.03342	78529	2625	386083	385728	3969513	50.55		
10 to 14	0.00403	0.01996	75904	1515	375733	375912	3583785	47.21	0.90883	0.90926
15 to 19	0.00443	0.02193	74389	921	369642	370095	3207873	43.12	0.95742	0.95947
20 to 24	0.00657	0.03236	73468	2377	361396	361675	2837778	38.63	0.96184	0.96213
25 to 29	0.00889	0.04355	71091	3096	347713	347946	2476103	34.83	0.94067	0.94016
30 to 34	0.01121	0.05463	67994	3714	330687	330870	2128157	31.30	0.91503	0.91483
35 to 39	0.01354	0.06563	64280	4219	310854	310984	1797287	27.96	0.89400	0.89377
40 to 44	0.01586	0.07647	60062	4593	288826	288901	1486304	24.75	0.87341	0.87316
45 to 49	0.01819	0.08724	55469	4839	265246	265636	1197403	21.59	0.85328	0.85418
50 to 54	0.02051	0.09784	50630	4954	240765	241481	931767	18.40	0.83360	0.83586
55 to 59	0.03156	0.14683	45676	6707	211614	212749	690286	15.11	0.79780	0.80091
60 to 64	0.04804	0.21535	38969	8392	173867	173415	477537	12.25	0.72215	0.71813
65 to 69	0.09933	0.39757	30577	12157	122496	120959	304123	9.95	0.57887	0.56855
70 to 74	0.08104	0.33760	18421	6219	76557	75945	183163	9.94	0.44032	0.43794
75 to 79	0.09750	0.39180	12202	4781	49058	48483	107219	8.79	0.40049	0.40083
80 to 84	0.11398	0.44197	7421	3280	28906	28665	58735	7.91	0.37758	0.37744
85 to 89	0.13046	0.48833	4141	2022	15651	15651	30071	7.26	0.31902	0.32280
90 +	0.14695	0.53117	2119	2119	14420	14420	14420	6.81	0.49885	0.50305

Table 3.10 : Total (Male and Female) Abridged Life table : Assam : 1961-71 (Set – 2)

Age	*Mx*	*qx*	*lx*	*dx*	*Lx*	*Lx1*	*Tx*	*ex*	*SR*	*SR1*
0-4	0.05598	0.24652	100000	24652	408096	408096	4416152			
0-	0.14600	0.14600	100000	14600	89430	89430	4416152	44.16		
1 to 4		0.09862	85400	8422	318666	318666	4326722	50.66		
5 to 9	0.00673	0.03313	76978	2551	378513	378173	4008056	52.07		
10 to 14	0.00362	0.01795	74427	1336	368797	368902	3629883	48.77	0.90370	0.90396
15 to 19	0.00351	0.01741	73091	921	363154	363448	3260981	44.62	0.95942	0.96106
20 to 24	0.00516	0.02550	72170	1840	356252	356446	2897534	40.15	0.96598	0.96624
25 to 29	0.00673	0.03313	70330	2330	345826	346017	2541088	36.13	0.95228	0.95204
30 to 34	0.00831	0.04076	68000	2772	333070	333401	2195070	32.28	0.93493	0.93535
35 to 39	0.01020	0.04982	65228	3250	318016	318425	1861669	28.54	0.91958	0.92026
40 to 44	0.01455	0.07036	61978	4361	298990	299285	1543244	24.90	0.89768	0.89767
45 to 49	0.01890	0.09050	57617	5214	275052	275409	1243959	21.59	0.86490	0.86491
50 to 54	0.02325	0.11023	52403	5776	247576	248287	968550	18.48	0.82804	0.82960
55 to 59	0.03197	0.14860	46627	6929	215814	216297	720263	15.45	0.78463	0.78537
60 to 64	0.05209	0.23139	39698	9186	175527	175198	503966	12.69	0.70898	0.70563
65 to 69	0.07119	0.30308	30512	9248	129443	128691	328768	10.77	0.59979	0.59497
70 to 74	0.08698	0.35765	21265	7605	87311	86500	200077	9.41	0.49742	0.49373
75 to 79	0.10417	0.41258	13659	5636	54208	53492	113577	8.31	0.41878	0.41566
80 to 84	0.12138	0.46324	8024	3717	30827	30492	60085	7.49	0.35307	0.35251
85 to 89	0.13859	0.50987	4307	2196	16044	16044	29593	6.87	0.29598	0.29994
90 +	0.15580	0.55278	2111	2111	13549	13549	13549	6.42	0.43952	0.44434

Table 3.11 : Male Abridged Life table : Assam : 1971-81 (Set – 1)

Age	Mx	qx	lx	dx	Lx	Lx1	Tx	ex	SR	SR1
0-4	0.0431	0.19536	100000	19536	420832	420832	4795676			
0-		0.13008	100000	13008	90582	90582	4795676	47.96		
1 to 4		0.07504	86992	6528	330250	330250	4705094	54.09		
5 to 9	0.0055	0.02730	80464	2197	396829	396563	4374844	54.37		
10 to 14	0.0028	0.01391	78267	1089	388615	388641	3978281	50.83	0.92345	0.92351
15 to 19	0.0019	0.00961	77179	921	383591	383696	3589640	46.51	0.96664	0.96755
20 to 24	0.0032	0.01588	76258	1211	378260	378325	3205944	42.04	0.97335	0.97346
25 to 29	0.0038	0.01898	75047	1425	371671	371819	2827620	37.68	0.96893	0.96905
30 to 34	0.0042	0.02065	73622	1520	364309	364891	2455801	33.36	0.96312	0.96449
35 to 39	0.006	0.02959	72102	2133	355174	355865	2090909	29.00	0.95561	0.95709
40 to 44	0.0127	0.06168	69968	4315	339053	339535	1735045	24.80	0.93067	0.93051
45 to 49	0.0173	0.08295	65653	5446	314649	315263	1395510	21.26	0.88590	0.88591
50 to 54	0.0232	0.11014	60207	6631	284456	285049	1080246	17.94	0.83897	0.83953
55 to 59	0.0339	0.15671	53576	8396	246889	247613	795198	14.84	0.78465	0.78542
60 to 64	0.0466	0.20969	45180	9474	202215	202211	547585	12.12	0.71088	0.70939
65 to 69	0.0795	0.33241	35706	11869	148858	147777	345374	9.67	0.60293	0.59681
70 to 74	0.099	0.39656	23837	9453	95553	94427	197597	8.29	0.47253	0.46697
75 to 79	0.1219	0.46457	14384	6682	55215	54264	103170	7.17	0.37092	0.36720
80 to 84	0.1447	0.52547	7702	4047	28391	27868	48906	6.35	0.29713	0.29513
85 to 89	0.1675	0.58001	3655	2120	12974	12974	21038	5.76	0.23498	0.23909
90 +	0.1904	0.62876	1535	1535	8064	8064	8064	5.25	0.28402	0.28936

Table 3.12 : Female Abridged Life table : Assam : 1971-81 (Set – 1)

Age	*Mx*	*qx*	*lx*	*Dx*	*Lx*	*Lx1*	*Tx*	*ex*	*SR*	*SR1*
0-4	0.0429	0.19454	100000	19454	422807	422807	4802931			
0-		0.12092	100000	12092	91245	91245	4802931	48.03		
1 to 4		0.08375	87908	7362	331561	331561	4711686	53.60		
5 to 9	0.0061	0.03022	80546	2434	396643	396328	4380125	54.38		
10 to 14	0.0033	0.01638	78112	1279	387360	387528	3983797	51.00	0.91616	0.91656
15 to 19	0.0037	0.01849	76832	921	381860	382255	3596269	46.81	0.96273	0.96449
20 to 24	0.0056	0.02750	75911	2087	374339	374517	3214013	42.34	0.96639	0.96643
25 to 29	0.0078	0.03821	73824	2821	362069	362128	2839496	38.46	0.94817	0.94735
30 to 34	0.0085	0.04144	71003	2942	347661	347117	2477368	34.89	0.92873	0.92684
35 to 39	0.0093	0.04561	68061	3104	332544	332624	2130251	31.30	0.91846	0.91853
40 to 44	0.001	0.00509	64957	331	323957	325233	1797627	27.67	0.93182	0.93696
45 to 49	0.0111	0.05396	64626	3487	314412	314964	1472394	22.78	0.94548	0.94691
50 to 54	0.0222	0.10564	61139	6458	289548	290345	1157429	18.93	0.89379	0.89273
55 to 59	0.0237	0.11224	54680	6138	258058	259216	867084	15.86	0.82076	0.82300
60 to 64	0.0472	0.21186	48543	10284	217003	216999	607868	12.52	0.74945	0.74738
65 to 69	0.0719	0.30573	38258	11697	162050	161173	390869	10.22	0.62796	0.62177
70 to 74	0.0958	0.38649	26562	10266	107144	105817	229696	8.65	0.49374	0.48764
75 to 79	0.12	0.45919	16296	7483	62772	61809	123879	7.60	0.38736	0.38349
80 to 84	0.1141	0.44220	8813	3897	34322	33939	62071	7.04	0.32034	0.32073
85 to 89	0.1682	0.58150	4916	2859	17433	17433	28132	5.72	0.27772	0.28205
90 +	0.1923	0.63266	2057	2057	10699	10699	10699	5.20	0.31172	0.31524

Table 3.13 : Total (Male and Female) Abridged Life table : Assam : 1971-81 (Set – 1)

Age	*Mx*	*qx*	*lx*	*Dx*	*Lx*	*Lx1*	*Tx*	*ex*	*SR*	*SR1*
0-4	0.0431	0.19524	100000	19524	421738	421738	4824264			
0-		0.12550	100000	12550	90914	90914	4824264	48.24		
1 to 4		0.07975	87450	6974	330825	330825	4733350	54.13		
5 to 9	0.0058	0.02876	80476	2315	396593	396302	4402526	54.71		
10 to 14	0.0031	0.01524	78161	1191	387828	387927	4006223	51.26	0.91959	0.91983
15 to 19	0.0028	0.01406	76970	921	382547	382798	3618296	47.01	0.96458	0.96593
20 to 24	0.0044	0.02193	76049	1667	376076	376198	3235498	42.54	0.96970	0.96977
25 to 29	0.0058	0.02862	74381	2128	366586	366730	2859300	38.44	0.95828	0.95802
30 to 34	0.0063	0.03119	72253	2254	355630	355237	2492570	34.50	0.94563	0.94428
35 to 39	0.0082	0.04028	69999	2820	342947	343389	2137333	30.53	0.93551	0.93635
40 to 44	0.0011	0.00544	67179	365	334984	336304	1793943	26.70	0.94194	0.94670
45 to 49	0.0153	0.07400	66814	4944	321710	322213	1457639	21.82	0.93808	0.93833
50 to 54	0.0228	0.10834	61870	6703	292592	293292	1135426	18.35	0.87345	0.87210
55 to 59	0.0285	0.13338	55167	7358	257439	258430	842134	15.27	0.80022	0.80205
60 to 64	0.0468	0.21050	47809	10063	213884	213893	583704	12.21	0.73100	0.72928
65 to 69	0.0762	0.32094	37745	12114	158441	157422	369811	9.80	0.61545	0.60915
70 to 74	0.0983	0.39423	25631	10105	102894	101703	212389	8.29	0.48107	0.47549
75 to 79	0.1222	0.46541	15526	7226	59567	58538	110686	7.13	0.37596	0.37186
80 to 84	0.146	0.52886	8300	4390	30527	29950	52147	6.28	0.29669	0.29449
85 to 89	0.1699	0.58538	3911	2289	13830	13830	22197	5.68	0.23218	0.23625
90 +	0.1938	0.63564	1621	1621	8367	8367	8367	5.16	0.27408	0.27936

Table 3.14 : Male Abridged Life table : Assam : 1971-81 (Set – 2)

Age	*Mx*	*qx*	*Lx*	*Dx*	*Lx*	*Lx1*	*Tx*	*ex*	*SR*	*SR1*
0-4	0.0431	0.19536	100000	19536	420832	420832	4813270			
0-		0.13008	100000	13008	90582	90582	4813270	48.13		
1 to 4		0.07504	86992	6528	330250	330250	4722688	54.29		
5 to 9	0.0055	0.02730	80464	2197	396829	396563	4392438	54.59		
10 to 14	0.0028	0.01391	78267	1089	388615	388641	3995875	51.05	0.92345	0.92351
15 to 19	0.0019	0.00961	77179	921	383591	383696	3607235	46.74	0.96664	0.96755
20 to 24	0.0032	0.01588	76258	1211	378260	378325	3223539	42.27	0.97335	0.97346
25 to 29	0.0038	0.01898	75047	1425	371671	371819	2845214	37.91	0.96893	0.96905
30 to 34	0.0042	0.02065	73622	1520	364309	364891	2473395	33.60	0.96312	0.96449
35 to 39	0.006	0.02959	72102	2133	355174	355865	2108504	29.24	0.95561	0.95709
40 to 44	0.0127	0.06168	69968	4315	339053	339535	1752639	25.05	0.93067	0.93051
45 to 49	0.0173	0.08295	65653	5446	314649	315263	1413104	21.52	0.88590	0.88591
50 to 54	0.0232	0.11014	60207	6631	284456	285049	1097841	18.23	0.83897	0.83953
55 to 59	0.0339	0.15671	53576	8396	246889	247613	812792	15.17	0.78465	0.78542
60 to 64	0.0466	0.20969	45180	9474	202215	202087	565179	12.51	0.71088	0.70896
65 to 69	0.0795	0.33241	35706	11869	148858	147722	363093	10.17	0.60293	0.59658
70 to 74	0.0912	0.37159	23837	8858	97041	96053	215371	9.04	0.47989	0.47531
75 to 79	0.1094	0.42833	14980	6416	58857	58010	119318	7.97	0.39539	0.39270
80 to 84	0.1275	0.48035	8563	4113	32533	32114	61308	7.16	0.33525	0.33433
85 to 89	0.1457	0.52801	4450	2350	16376	16376	29194	6.56	0.27823	0.28229
90 +	0.1639	0.57165	2100	2100	12819	12819	12819	6.10	0.39401	0.39916

Table 3.15 : Female Abridged Life table : Assam : 1971-81 (Set – 2)

Age	*Mx*	*qx*	*Lx*	*dx*	*Lx*	*Lx1*	*Tx*	*ex*	*SR*	*SR1*
0-4	0.0429	0.19454	100000	19454	422807	422807	4828072			
0-		0.12092	100000	12092	91245	91245	4828072	48.28		
1 to 4		0.08375	87908	7362	331561	331561	4736826	53.88		
5 to 9	0.0061	0.03022	80546	2434	396643	396328	4405265	54.69		
10 to 14	0.0033	0.01638	78112	1279	387360	387528	4008937	51.32	0.91616	0.91656
15 to 19	0.0037	0.01849	76832	921	381860	382255	3621409	47.13	0.96273	0.96449
20 to 24	0.0056	0.02750	75911	2087	374339	374517	3239154	42.67	0.96639	0.96643
25 to 29	0.0078	0.03821	73824	2821	362069	362128	2864636	38.80	0.94817	0.94735
30 to 34	0.0085	0.04144	71003	2942	347661	347117	2502509	35.24	0.92873	0.92684
35 to 39	0.0093	0.04561	68061	3104	332544	332624	2155392	31.67	0.91846	0.91853
40 to 44	0.001	0.00509	64957	331	323957	325233	1822768	28.06	0.93182	0.93696
45 to 49	0.0111	0.05396	64626	3487	314412	314964	1497534	23.17	0.94548	0.94691
50 to 54	0.0222	0.10564	61139	6458	289548	290345	1182570	19.34	0.89379	0.89273
55 to 59	0.0237	0.11224	54680	6138	258058	259216	892225	16.32	0.82076	0.82300
60 to 64	0.0472	0.21186	48543	10284	217003	216792	633009	13.04	0.74945	0.74667
65 to 69	0.0719	0.30573	38258	11697	162050	161072	416217	10.88	0.62796	0.62138
70 to 74	0.0844	0.34898	26562	9269	109635	108682	255145	9.61	0.50522	0.50132
75 to 79	0.1017	0.40481	17292	7000	68961	68090	146463	8.47	0.42556	0.42273
80 to 84	0.1189	0.45622	10292	4696	39722	39323	78372	7.61	0.36231	0.36182
85 to 89	0.1362	0.50352	5597	2818	20938	20938	39050	6.98	0.30362	0.30751
90 +	0.1534	0.54706	2779	2779	18111	18111	18111	6.52	0.45595	0.46058

Table 3.16 : Total (Male and Female) Abridged Life table : Assam : 1971-81 (Set – 2)

Age	*Mx*	*qx*	*lx*	*dx*	*Lx*	*Lx1*	*Tx*	*ex*	*SR*	*SR1*
0-4	0.0431	0.19524	100000	19524	421738	421738	4850445			
0-		0.12550	100000	12550	90914	90914	4850445	48.50		
1 to 4		0.07975	87450	6974	330825	330825	4759531	54.43		
5 to 9	0.0058	0.02876	80476	2315	396593	396302	4428707	55.03		
10 to 14	0.0031	0.01524	78161	1191	387828	387927	4032404	51.59	0.91959	0.91983
15 to 19	0.0028	0.01406	76970	921	382547	382798	3644477	47.35	0.96458	0.96593
20 to 24	0.0044	0.02193	76049	1667	376076	376198	3261679	42.89	0.96970	0.96977
25 to 29	0.0058	0.02862	74381	2128	366586	366730	2885481	38.79	0.95828	0.95802
30 to 34	0.0063	0.03119	72253	2254	355630	355237	2518751	34.86	0.94563	0.94428
35 to 39	0.0082	0.04028	69999	2820	342947	343389	2163514	30.91	0.93551	0.93635
40 to 44	0.0011	0.00544	67179	365	334984	336304	1820124	27.09	0.94194	0.94670
45 to 49	0.0153	0.07400	66814	4944	321710	322213	1483820	22.21	0.93808	0.93833
50 to 54	0.0228	0.10834	61870	6703	292592	293292	1161607	18.78	0.87345	0.87210
55 to 59	0.0285	0.13338	55167	7358	257439	258430	868315	15.74	0.80022	0.80205
60 to 64	0.0468	0.21050	47809	10063	213884	213708	609885	12.76	0.73100	0.72865
65 to 69	0.0762	0.32094	37745	12114	158441	157341	396177	10.50	0.61545	0.60883
70 to 74	0.0876	0.35961	25631	9217	105112	104127	238836	9.32	0.49145	0.48724
75 to 79	0.1054	0.41643	16414	6835	64981	64105	134709	8.21	0.41013	0.40743
80 to 84	0.1233	0.46861	9579	4489	36671	36249	70604	7.37	0.34888	0.34812
85 to 89	0.1412	0.51649	5090	2629	18878	18878	34355	6.75	0.29051	0.29448
90 +	0.159	0.56040	2461	2461	15478	15478	15478	6.29	0.42206	0.42698

Table 3.17 : Male Abridged Life table : Assam : 1981-91 (Set – 1)

Age	*Mx*	*qx*	*lx*	*dx*	*Lx*	*Lx1*	*Tx*	*ex*	*SR*	*SR1*
0-4	0.0369	0.16974	100000	16974	433794	433794	5189996			
0-		0.09950	100000	9950	92796	92796	5189996	51.90		
1 to 4		0.07800	90050	7024	340998	340998	5097200	56.60		
5 to 9	0.0038	0.01898	83026	1576	411190	411054	4756202	57.29		
10 to 14	0.0025	0.01258	81450	1024	404690	404720	4345148	53.35	0.93291	0.93298
15 to 19	0.0023	0.01144	80426	921	399826	399928	3940427	48.99	0.97236	0.97293
20 to 24	0.0030	0.01475	79505	1173	394592	394694	3540499	44.53	0.97505	0.97523
25 to 29	0.0036	0.01800	78332	1410	388136	388201	3145805	40.16	0.97076	0.97068
30 to 34	0.0044	0.02163	76922	1664	380451	380682	2757603	35.85	0.96416	0.96450
35 to 39	0.0046	0.02290	75258	1724	371982	372432	2376922	31.58	0.95838	0.95938
40 to 44	0.0077	0.03768	73534	2771	360746	361693	2004489	27.26	0.94820	0.95012
45 to 49	0.0113	0.05491	70764	3886	344104	344870	1642797	23.22	0.92506	0.92599
50 to 54	0.0231	0.10942	66878	7318	316096	316647	1297927	19.41	0.87623	0.87546
55 to 59	0.0270	0.12692	59560	7559	278904	279809	981280	16.49	0.81052	0.81135
60 to 64	0.0422	0.19155	52001	9961	235104	235204	701472	13.49	0.74377	0.74280
65 to 69	0.0657	0.28313	42041	11903	180445	179644	466267	11.09	0.64698	0.64202
70 to 74	0.0837	0.34651	30138	10443	124580	123534	286624	9.51	0.52989	0.52522
75 to 79	0.1030	0.40902	19695	8055	78334	77327	163089	8.28	0.43412	0.43044
80 to 84	0.1224	0.46600	11639	5424	44636	44130	85763	7.37	0.35829	0.35723
85 to 89	0.1417	0.51792	6215	3219	23029	23029	41632	6.70	0.29398	0.29781
90 +	0.1611	0.56520	2996	2996	18603	18603	18603	6.21	0.41678	0.42156

Table 3.18 : Female Abridged Life table : Assam : 1981-91 (Set – 1)

Age	*Mx*	*qx*	*lx*	*dx*	*Lx*	*Lx1*	*Tx*	*ex*	*SR*	*SR1*
0-4	0.0380	0.17411	100000	17411	434665	434665	5140398			
0-		0.09250	100000	9250	93303	93303	5140398	51.40		
1 to 4		0.08695	90750	7891	341362	341362	5047095	55.62		
5 to 9	0.0055	0.02715	82859	2250	408670	408393	4705733	56.79		
10 to 14	0.0027	0.01327	80609	1070	400371	400548	4297340	53.31	0.92110	0.92151
15 to 19	0.0029	0.01440	79539	921	395395	395647	3896792	48.99	0.96752	0.96879
20 to 24	0.0049	0.02437	78618	1916	388302	388430	3501145	44.53	0.96986	0.96975
25 to 29	0.0056	0.02779	76702	2131	378183	378279	3112715	40.58	0.95647	0.95610
30 to 34	0.0069	0.03391	74571	2529	366533	366573	2734437	36.67	0.94394	0.94373
35 to 39	0.0073	0.03594	72042	2589	353739	353763	2367864	32.87	0.93536	0.93519
40 to 44	0.0080	0.03913	69453	2717	340472	340973	2014101	29.00	0.92890	0.93017
45 to 49	0.0083	0.04052	66736	2704	326917	327597	1673128	25.07	0.92418	0.92604
50 to 54	0.0166	0.08004	64031	5125	307343	308279	1345532	21.01	0.90270	0.90411
55 to 59	0.0213	0.10129	58906	5967	279614	280673	1037253	17.61	0.85530	0.85677
60 to 64	0.0398	0.18162	52939	9615	240659	240825	756579	14.29	0.78303	0.78119
65 to 69	0.0582	0.25515	43324	11054	188986	188434	515754	11.90	0.67588	0.67137
70 to 74	0.0767	0.32266	32270	10412	135321	134388	327320	10.14	0.56229	0.55803
75 to 79	0.0952	0.38448	21858	8404	88280	87302	192931	8.83	0.46713	0.46330
80 to 84	0.1137	0.44115	13454	5935	52432	51990	105630	7.85	0.38747	0.38687
85 to 89	0.1322	0.49290	7519	3706	28329	28329	53640	7.13	0.32090	0.32450
90 +	0.1506	0.54029	3813	3813	25311	25311	25311	6.64	0.48273	0.48683

Table 3.19 : Total (Male and Female) Abridged Life table : Assam : 1981-91 (Set – 1)

Age	*Mx*	*qx*	*lx*	*dx*	*Lx*	*Lx1*	*Tx*	*ex*	*SR*	*SR1*
0-4	0.0374	0.17184	100000	17184	433801	433801	5157127			
0-		0.09640	100000	9640	93021	93021	5157127	51.57		
1 to 4		0.08349	90360	7544	340780	340780	5064106	56.04		
5 to 9	0.0044	0.02158	82816	1787	409611	409430	4723326	57.03		
10 to 14	0.0026	0.01292	81028	1047	402525	402633	4313896	53.24	0.92790	0.92815
15 to 19	0.0026	0.01292	79981	921	397604	397782	3911263	48.90	0.97069	0.97155
20 to 24	0.0040	0.01982	79060	1567	391385	391477	3513481	44.44	0.97233	0.97229
25 to 29	0.0046	0.02290	77494	1775	383031	383142	3122004	40.29	0.96335	0.96319
30 to 34	0.0054	0.02652	75719	2008	373573	373692	2738862	36.17	0.95449	0.95457
35 to 39	0.0064	0.03129	73711	2306	362787	363007	2365171	32.09	0.94715	0.94745
40 to 44	0.0073	0.03609	71404	2577	350579	351362	2002164	28.04	0.93845	0.94025
45 to 49	0.0100	0.04886	68827	3363	335729	336454	1650802	23.98	0.92542	0.92685
50 to 54	0.0203	0.09675	65464	6334	311487	312206	1314348	20.08	0.88849	0.88856
55 to 59	0.0245	0.11569	59130	6841	278550	279527	1002143	16.95	0.82969	0.83080
60 to 64	0.0411	0.18714	52290	9785	236985	237118	722616	13.82	0.76082	0.75949
65 to 69	0.0625	0.27126	42504	11530	183697	183003	485497	11.42	0.65948	0.65469
70 to 74	0.0807	0.33650	30975	10423	128815	127817	302494	9.77	0.54356	0.53904
75 to 79	0.0997	0.39885	20552	8197	82265	81269	174677	8.50	0.44783	0.44408
80 to 84	0.1188	0.45577	12354	5631	47696	47212	93409	7.56	0.37026	0.36937
85 to 89	0.1378	0.50771	6724	3414	25084	25084	46197	6.87	0.30492	0.30866
90 +	0.1568	0.55512	3310	3310	21112	21112	21112	6.38	0.44265	0.44718

Table 3.20 : Male Abridged Life table : Assam : 1981-91 (Set – 2)

Age	*Mx*	*qx*	*lx*	*dx*	*Lx*	*Lx1*	*Tx*	*ex*	*SR*	*SR1*
0-4	0.0369	0.16974	100000	16974	433794	433794	5224918			
0-		0.09950	100000	9950	92796	92796	5224918	52.25		
1 to 4		0.07800	90050	7024	340998	340998	5132121	56.99		
5 to 9	0.0038	0.01898	83026	1576	411190	411054	4791124	57.71		
10 to 14	0.0025	0.01258	81450	1024	404690	404720	4380070	53.78	0.93291	0.93298
15 to 19	0.0023	0.01144	80426	921	399826	399928	3975349	49.43	0.97236	0.97293
20 to 24	0.003	0.01475	79505	1173	394592	394694	3575421	44.97	0.97505	0.97523
25 to 29	0.0036	0.01800	78332	1410	388136	388201	3180727	40.61	0.97076	0.97068
30 to 34	0.0044	0.02163	76922	1664	380451	380682	2792525	36.30	0.96416	0.96450
35 to 39	0.0046	0.02290	75258	1724	371982	372432	2411844	32.05	0.95838	0.95938
40 to 44	0.0077	0.03768	73534	2771	360746	361693	2039411	27.73	0.94820	0.95012
45 to 49	0.0113	0.05491	70764	3886	344104	344870	1677719	23.71	0.92506	0.92599
50 to 54	0.0231	0.10942	66878	7318	316096	316647	1332849	19.93	0.87623	0.87546
55 to 59	0.027	0.12692	59560	7559	278904	279809	1016202	17.06	0.81052	0.81135
60 to 64	0.0422	0.19155	52001	9961	235104	235022	736394	14.16	0.74377	0.74222
65 to 69	0.0657	0.28313	42041	11903	180445	179534	501371	11.93	0.64698	0.64163
70 to 74	0.0753	0.31750	30138	9569	126766	125890	321837	10.68	0.53919	0.53565
75 to 79	0.0896	0.36618	20569	7532	84014	83171	195947	9.53	0.46559	0.46326
80 to 84	0.1039	0.41163	13037	5366	51768	51523	112776	8.65	0.40838	0.40927
85 to 89	0.1182	0.45411	7670	3483	29644	29644	61254	7.99	0.35285	0.35643
90 +	0.1325	0.49373	4187	4187	31609	31609	31609	7.55	0.61059	0.61350

Table 3.21 : Female Abridged Life table : Assam : 1981-91 (Set – 2)

Age	*Mx*	*qx*	*lx*	*dx*	*Lx*	*Lx1*	*Tx*	*ex*	*SR*	*SR1*
0-4	0.038	0.17411	100000	17411	434665	434665	5175482			
0-		0.09250	100000	9250	93303	93303	5175482	51.75		
1 to 4		0.08695	90750	7891	341362	341362	5082179	56.00		
5 to 9	0.0055	0.02715	82859	2250	408670	408393	4740817	57.22		
10 to 14	0.0027	0.01327	80609	1070	400371	400548	4332424	53.75	0.92110	0.92151
15 to 19	0.0029	0.01440	79539	921	395395	395647	3931877	49.43	0.96752	0.96879
20 to 24	0.0049	0.02437	78618	1916	388302	388430	3536230	44.98	0.96986	0.96975
25 to 29	0.0056	0.02779	76702	2131	378183	378279	3147800	41.04	0.95647	0.95610
30 to 34	0.0069	0.03391	74571	2529	366533	366573	2769521	37.14	0.94394	0.94373
35 to 39	0.0073	0.03594	72042	2589	353739	353763	2402948	33.35	0.93536	0.93519
40 to 44	0.008	0.03913	69453	2717	340472	340973	2049186	29.50	0.92890	0.93017
45 to 49	0.0083	0.04052	66736	2704	326917	327597	1708213	25.60	0.92418	0.92604
50 to 54	0.0166	0.08004	64031	5125	307343	308279	1380616	21.56	0.90270	0.90411
55 to 59	0.0213	0.10129	58906	5967	279614	280673	1072337	18.20	0.85530	0.85677
60 to 64	0.0398	0.18162	52939	9615	240659	240660	791664	14.95	0.78303	0.78066
65 to 69	0.0582	0.25515	43324	11054	188986	188326	551004	12.72	0.67588	0.67098
70 to 74	0.0698	0.29808	32270	9619	137304	136515	362677	11.24	0.57053	0.56725
75 to 79	0.0841	0.34810	22651	7885	93544	92718	226163	9.98	0.49498	0.49232
80 to 84	0.0985	0.39483	14766	5830	59256	59087	133445	9.04	0.43157	0.43283
85 to 89	0.1128	0.43848	8936	3918	34885	34885	74358	8.32	0.37293	0.37625
90 +	0.1271	0.47923	5018	5018	39473	39473	39473	7.87	0.66615	0.66805

Table 3.22 : Total (Male and Female) Abridged Life table : Assam : 1981-91 (Set – 2)

Age	*Mx*	*Qx*	*lx*	*dx*	*Lx*	*Lx1*	*Tx*	*ex*	*SR*	*SR1*
0-4	0.0374	0.17184	100000	17184	433801	433801	5191684			
0-		0.09640	100000	9640	93021	93021	5191684	51.92		
1 to 4		0.08349	90360	7544	340780	340780	5098663	56.43		
5 to 9	0.0044	0.02158	82816	1787	409611	409430	4757883	57.45		
10 to 14	0.0026	0.01292	81028	1047	402525	402633	4348453	53.67	0.92790	0.92815
15 to 19	0.0026	0.01292	79981	921	397604	397782	3945820	49.33	0.97069	0.97155
20 to 24	0.004	0.01982	79060	1567	391385	391477	3548038	44.88	0.97233	0.97229
25 to 29	0.0046	0.02290	77494	1775	383031	383142	3156561	40.73	0.96335	0.96319
30 to 34	0.0054	0.02652	75719	2008	373573	373692	2773419	36.63	0.95449	0.95457
35 to 39	0.0064	0.03129	73711	2306	362787	363007	2399728	32.56	0.94715	0.94745
40 to 44	0.0073	0.03609	71404	2577	350579	351362	2036721	28.52	0.93845	0.94025
45 to 49	0.01	0.04886	68827	3363	335729	336454	1685359	24.49	0.92542	0.92685
50 to 54	0.0203	0.09675	65464	6334	311487	312206	1348905	20.61	0.88849	0.88856
55 to 59	0.0245	0.11569	59130	6841	278550	279527	1036700	17.53	0.82969	0.83080
60 to 64	0.0411	0.18714	52290	9785	236985	236946	757172	14.48	0.76082	0.75894
65 to 69	0.0625	0.27126	42504	11530	183697	182895	520226	12.24	0.65948	0.65430
70 to 74	0.0731	0.30983	30975	9597	130881	130038	337331	10.89	0.55227	0.54881
75 to 79	0.0874	0.35918	21378	7678	87693	86854	207293	9.70	0.47738	0.47488
80 to 84	0.1018	0.40527	13699	5552	54617	54396	120439	8.79	0.41730	0.41831
85 to 89	0.1162	0.44831	8147	3653	31605	31605	66043	8.11	0.36041	0.36389
90 +	0.1305	0.48849	4495	4495	34437	34437	34437	7.66	0.63053	0.63308

Table 3.23 : Male Abridged Life table : Assam : 1971-91 (Set – 1)

Age	*Mx*	*Qx*	*lx*	*dx*	*Lx*	*Lx1*	*Tx*	*ex*	*SR*	*SR1*
0-4	0.0407	0.18540	100000	18540	426519	426519	4952249			
0-		0.11479	100000	11479	91689	91689	4952249	49.52		
1 to 4		0.07977	88521	7061	334830	334830	4860560	54.91		
5 to 9	0.0049	0.02442	81460	1989	402325	402103	4525731	55.56		
10 to 14	0.0026	0.01272	79470	1011	394824	394855	4123628	51.89		
15 to 19	0.0021	0.01045	78459	921	389993	390071	3728773	47.53		
20 to 24	0.0030	0.01500	77538	1163	384784	384832	3338702	43.06	0.90215	0.90226
25 to 29	0.0034	0.01697	76375	1296	378637	378890	2953869	38.68	0.94112	0.94227
30 to 34	0.0038	0.01859	75080	1396	371909	372347	2574980	34.30	0.94196	0.94300
35 to 39	0.0069	0.03401	73684	2506	362156	362659	2202633	29.89	0.92862	0.92973
40 to 44	0.0101	0.04915	71178	3499	347145	347783	1839974	25.85	0.90218	0.90373
45 to 49	0.0151	0.07274	67680	4923	326091	326724	1492191	22.05	0.86122	0.86232
50 to 54	0.0220	0.10451	62756	6558	297386	298042	1165467	18.57	0.79962	0.80044
55 to 59	0.0304	0.14172	56198	7964	261080	261952	867425	15.44	0.72090	0.72231
60 to 64	0.0445	0.20123	48234	9706	216903	216975	605473	12.55	0.62482	0.62388
65 to 69	0.0747	0.31542	38528	12153	162256	161251	388498	10.08	0.49758	0.49354
70 to 74	0.0941	0.38108	26375	10051	106748	105609	227246	8.62	0.35895	0.35434
75 to 79	0.1164	0.44889	16324	7328	63301	62293	121638	7.45	0.24246	0.23780
80 to 84	0.1384	0.50943	8996	4583	33524	32970	59345	6.60	0.15456	0.15195
85 to 89	0.1606	0.56403	4413	2489	15843	15843	26375	5.98	0.09764	0.09825
90 +	0.1827	0.61303	1924	1924	10531	10531	10531	5.47	0.09866	0.09972

Table 3.24 : Female Abridged Life table : Assam : 1971-91 (Set – 1)

Age	*Mx*	*qx*	*lx*	*dx*	*Lx*	*Lx1*	*Tx*	*ex*	*SR*	*SR1*
0-4	0.0401	0.18283	100000	18283	428782	428782	4926249			
0-		0.10670	100000	10670	92275	92275	4926249	49.26		
1 to 4		0.08521	89330	7612	336507	336507	4833974	54.11		
5 to 9	0.0060	0.02949	81718	2410	402566	402256	4497467	55.04		
10 to 14	0.0030	0.01500	79308	1189	393568	393747	4095211	51.64		
15 to 19	0.0035	0.01716	78119	921	388292	388639	3701464	47.38		
20 to 24	0.0054	0.02657	77198	2051	380862	380981	3312825	42.91	0.88824	0.88852
25 to 29	0.0070	0.03444	75147	2588	369264	369304	2931844	39.01	0.91728	0.91808
30 to 34	0.0074	0.03613	72559	2622	356239	356272	2562540	35.32	0.90515	0.90482
35 to 39	0.0081	0.03975	69937	2780	342733	342784	2206268	31.55	0.88267	0.88201
40 to 44	0.0085	0.04144	67157	2783	328826	329454	1863484	27.75	0.86337	0.86475
45 to 49	0.0096	0.04695	64374	3023	314312	314892	1534030	23.83	0.85119	0.85266
50 to 54	0.0198	0.09452	61351	5799	292259	293075	1219138	19.87	0.82040	0.82262
55 to 59	0.0220	0.10451	55552	5806	263248	264368	926063	16.67	0.76808	0.77124
60 to 64	0.0431	0.19536	49747	9719	224437	224541	661695	13.30	0.68254	0.68156
65 to 69	0.0647	0.27937	40028	11183	172185	171493	437154	10.92	0.54781	0.54461
70 to 74	0.0860	0.35421	28846	10217	118684	117640	265661	9.21	0.40609	0.40140
75 to 79	0.1073	0.42211	18628	7863	73483	72469	148021	7.95	0.27914	0.27412
80 to 84	0.1287	0.48341	10765	5204	40815	40266	75552	7.02	0.18186	0.17932
85 to 89	0.1500	0.53872	5561	2996	20316	20316	35286	6.35	0.11799	0.11846
90 +	0.1714	0.58858	2565	2565	14971	14971	14971	5.84	0.12614	0.12726

Table 3.25 : Total (Male and Female) Abridged Life table : Assam : 1971-91 (Set – 1)

Age	*Mx*	*qx*	*lx*	*Dx*	*Lx*	*Lx1*	*Tx*	*ex*	*SR*	*SR1*
0-4	0.0404	0.18424	100000	18424	427574	427574	4991407			
0-		0.11095	100000	11095	91967	91967	4991407	49.91		
1 to 4		0.08244	88905	7329	335607	335607	4899440	55.11		
5 to 9	0.0054	0.02686	81576	2191	402400	402136	4563833	55.95		
10 to 14	0.0028	0.01391	79384	1104	394161	394271	4161698	52.42		
15 to 19	0.0028	0.01381	78280	921	389098	389316	3767426	48.13		
20 to 24	0.0043	0.02109	77359	1632	382717	382813	3378110	43.67	0.89509	0.89531
25 to 29	0.0053	0.02598	75727	1968	373718	373848	2995298	39.55	0.92872	0.92966
30 to 34	0.0058	0.02837	73760	2093	363567	363763	2621449	35.54	0.92238	0.92262
35 to 39	0.0074	0.03618	71667	2593	351852	352184	2257686	31.50	0.90428	0.90462
40 to 44	0.0090	0.04394	69074	3035	337783	338128	1905502	27.59	0.88259	0.88327
45 to 49	0.0131	0.06337	66039	4185	319733	320644	1567374	23.73	0.85555	0.85769
50 to 54	0.0157	0.07591	61854	4695	297532	298763	1246729	20.16	0.81837	0.82131
55 to 59	0.0322	0.14976	57159	8560	264393	264838	947966	16.58	0.75143	0.75199
60 to 64	0.0488	0.21818	48599	10603	216484	216377	683128	14.06	0.64090	0.63993
65 to 69	0.0653	0.28147	37995	10695	163239	161208	466751	12.28	0.51055	0.50276
70 to 74	0.0906	0.36953	27301	10088	111282	110869	305544	11.19	0.37402	0.37109
75 to 79	0.0112	0.05475	17212	942	83705	84450	194675	11.31	0.31659	0.31887
80 to 84	0.1341	0.49818	16270	8105	61986	60157	110225	6.77	0.28217	0.27802
85 to 89	0.1559	0.55307	8164	4516	29534	29534	50068	6.13	0.18092	0.18320
90 +	0.1777	0.60243	3649	3649	20534	20534	20534	5.63	0.18453	0.18521

Table 3.26 : Male Abridged Life table : Assam : 1971-91 (Set – 2)

Age	*Mx*	*qx*	*lx*	*dx*	*Lx*	*Lx1*	*Tx*	*ex*	*SR*	*SR1*
0-4	0.0407	0.18540	100000	18540	427712	427712	5408209			
0-		0.10854	100000	10854	92142	92142	4980497	49.80		
1 to 4		0.08622	89146	7686	335570	335570	4888355	54.84		
5 to 9	0.0049	0.02442	81460	1989	402326	402082	4552785	55.89		
10 to 14	0.0026	0.01272	79470	1011	394824	394856	4150703	52.23		
15 to 19	0.0021	0.01045	78459	820	390247	390346	3755847	47.87		
20 to 24	0.0030	0.01500	77639	1164	385286	385335	3365500	43.35	0.90081	0.90092
25 to 29	0.0034	0.01697	76475	1297	379132	379384	2980165	38.97	0.94235	0.94355
30 to 34	0.0038	0.01859	75178	1397	372395	372833	2600781	34.60	0.94319	0.94423
35 to 39	0.0069	0.03401	73780	2509	362629	363133	2227948	30.20	0.92923	0.93028
40 to 44	0.0101	0.04915	71271	3503	347599	348237	1864815	26.17	0.90218	0.90373
45 to 49	0.0151	0.07274	67768	4930	326517	327151	1516578	22.38	0.86122	0.86232
50 to 54	0.0220	0.10451	62838	6567	297775	298431	1189427	18.93	0.79962	0.80044
55 to 59	0.0304	0.14172	56271	7975	261421	262294	890995	15.83	0.72090	0.72231
60 to 64	0.0445	0.20123	48297	9719	217187	217111	628701	13.02	0.62482	0.62346
65 to 69	0.0747	0.31542	38578	12168	162468	161388	411590	10.67	0.49758	0.49331
70 to 74	0.0859	0.35418	26409	9354	108663	107681	250202	9.47	0.36492	0.36082
75 to 79	0.1032	0.40948	17056	6984	67819	66938	142521	8.36	0.25942	0.25520
80 to 84	0.1204	0.46041	10072	4637	38766	38347	75583	7.50	0.17849	0.17662
85 to 89	0.1376	0.50730	5435	2757	20281	20281	37236	6.85	0.12483	0.12567
90 +	0.1548	0.55043	2678	2625	16955	16955	16955	6.33	0.15603	0.15746

Table 3.27 : Female Abridged Life table : Assam : 1971-91 (Set – 2)

Age	*Mx*	*qx*	*lx*	*dx*	*Lx*	*Lx1*	*Tx*	*ex*	*SR*	*SR1*
0-4	0.0401	0.18283	100000	18283	428782	428782	4961526			
0-		0.10670	100000	10670	92275	92275	4961526	49.62		
1 to 4		0.08521	89330	7612	336507	336507	4869251	54.51		
5 to 9	0.0060	0.02949	81718	2410	402566	402256	4532745	55.47		
10 to 14	0.0030	0.01500	79308	1189	393568	393747	4130489	52.08		
15 to 19	0.0035	0.01716	78119	921	388292	388639	3736742	47.83		
20 to 24	0.0054	0.02657	77198	2051	380862	380981	3348102	43.37	0.88824	0.88852
25 to 29	0.0070	0.03444	75147	2588	369264	369304	2967122	39.48	0.91728	0.91808
30 to 34	0.0074	0.03613	72559	2622	356239	356272	2597818	35.80	0.90515	0.90482
35 to 39	0.0081	0.03975	69937	2780	342733	342784	2241546	32.05	0.88267	0.88201
40 to 44	0.0085	0.04144	67157	2783	328826	329454	1898762	28.27	0.86337	0.86475
45 to 49	0.0096	0.04695	64374	3023	314312	314892	1569308	24.38	0.85119	0.85266
50 to 54	0.0198	0.09452	61351	5799	292259	293075	1254416	20.45	0.82040	0.82262
55 to 59	0.0220	0.10451	55552	5806	263248	264368	961340	17.31	0.76808	0.77124
60 to 64	0.0431	0.19536	49747	9719	224437	224343	696973	14.01	0.68254	0.68096
65 to 69	0.0647	0.27937	40028	11183	172185	171380	472629	11.81	0.54781	0.54425
70 to 74	0.0763	0.32129	28846	9268	121058	120207	301249	10.44	0.41422	0.41016
75 to 79	0.0919	0.37390	19578	7320	79588	78753	181042	9.25	0.30233	0.29789
80 to 84	0.1075	0.42271	12258	5181	48335	48039	102289	8.34	0.21536	0.21413
85 to 89	0.1231	0.46802	7076	3312	27101	27101	54250	7.67	0.15740	0.15814
90 +	0.1387	0.51006	3764	3764	27148	27148	27148	7.21	0.22426	0.22585

Table 3.28 : Total (Male and Female) Abridged Life table : Assam : 1971-91 (Set – 2)

Age	*Mx*	*qx*	*lx*	*dx*	*Lx*	*Lx1*	*Tx*	*ex*	*SR*	*SR1*
0-4	0.0404	0.18424	100000	18424	427574	427574	4956733			
0-		0.11095	100000	11095	91967	91967	4956733	49.57		
1 to 4		0.08244	88905	7329	335607	335607	4864766	54.72		
5 to 9	0.0054	0.02686	81576	2191	402400	402136	4529159	55.52		
10 to 14	0.0028	0.01391	79384	1104	394161	394271	4127024	51.99		
15 to 19	0.0028	0.01381	78280	921	389098	389316	3732752	47.68		
20 to 24	0.0043	0.02109	77359	1632	382717	382813	3343436	43.22	0.89509	0.89531
25 to 29	0.0053	0.02598	75727	1968	373718	373848	2960623	39.10	0.92872	0.92966
30 to 34	0.0058	0.02837	73760	2093	363567	363763	2586775	35.07	0.92238	0.92262
35 to 39	0.0074	0.03618	71667	2593	351852	352184	2223012	31.02	0.90428	0.90462
40 to 44	0.0090	0.04394	69074	3035	337783	338128	1870828	27.08	0.88259	0.88327
45 to 49	0.0131	0.06337	66039	4185	319733	320644	1532699	23.21	0.85555	0.85769
50 to 54	0.0157	0.07591	61854	4695	297532	298763	1212055	19.60	0.81837	0.82131
55 to 59	0.0322	0.14976	57159	8560	264393	264838	913292	15.98	0.75143	0.75199
60 to 64	0.0488	0.21818	48599	10603	216484	216209	648454	13.34	0.64090	0.63943
65 to 69	0.0653	0.28147	37995	10695	163239	162491	432245	11.38	0.51055	0.50676
70 to 74	0.0818	0.34002	27301	9283	113296	112372	269754	9.88	0.38078	0.37612
75 to 79	0.0983	0.39417	18018	7102	72333	71474	157382	8.73	0.27358	0.26988
80 to 84	0.1148	0.44422	10916	4849	42456	42090	85909	7.87	0.19612	0.19467
85 to 89	0.1312	0.49043	6067	2975	22895	22895	43819	7.22	0.14026	0.14090
90 +	0.1478	0.53316	3091	3091	20923	20923	20923	6.77	0.18468	0.18620

Table 3.29 : Male Abridged Life table : Assam : 1951-61

Age group	*qx*	*Lx*	*dx*	*Lx*	*Tx*	*ex*	*SR*
0 - 1	0.207000	100000	20700	85013	3684174	36.842	
1 – 4	0.129564	79300	10274	289320	3599161	45.387	
5 – 9	0.051008	69026	3521	335899	3309841	47.951	
10 – 14	0.019840	65505	1300	324369	2973942	45.400	0.86653
15 – 19	0.022959	64205	1474	317485	2649573	41.267	0.94518
20 – 24	0.027982	62731	1755	309473	2332089	37.176	0.95408
25 – 29	0.035563	60976	2168	299724	2022616	33.171	0.94406
30 –34	0.046719	58807	2747	287484	1722893	29.297	0.92895
35 – 39	0.061543	56060	3450	272027	1435410	25.605	0.90759
40 – 44	0.081089	52610	4266	252787	1163384	22.113	0.87931
45 – 49	0.106404	48344	5144	229347	910597	18.836	0.84310
50 – 54	0.143579	43200	6203	200821	681251	15.770	0.79443
55 – 59	0.202350	36997	7486	166276	480430	12.986	0.72495
60 – 64	0.263664	29511	7781	127798	314154	10.645	0.63638
65 – 69	0.345890	21730	7516	89210	186355	8.576	0.53652
70 – 74	0.444954	14214	6324	54432	97145	6.835	0.42592
75 – 79	0.558008	7889	4402	27758	42713	5.414	0.31115
80 – 84	0.677721	3487	2363	11527	14955	4.289	0.21177
85 +	1.000000	1124	1124	3428	3428	3.051	0.12350

Source : K.L. Kohli, *Mortality in India*, 1977, pp. 228-229.
Values of SRs are derived from the Lxs.

Table 3.30 : Female Abridged Life table : Assam : 1951-61

Age group	*qx*	*lx*	*dx*	*Lx*	*Tx*	*ex*	*SR*
0 - 1	0.161000	100000	16100	88344	3621770	36.218	
1 – 4	0.107339	83900	9006	311093	3533427	42.115	
5 – 9	0.051585	74894	3863	364577	3222334	43.025	
10 – 14	0.026328	71031	1870	350823	2857758	40.233	0.87829
15 – 19	0.039482	69161	2731	339279	2506935	36.248	0.93061
20 – 24	0.053040	66430	3523	323593	2167656	36.631	0.92238
25 – 29	0.066496	6290	4183	304285	1844063	29.314	0.89685
30 –34	0.080557	58724	4731	281964	1539779	26.221	0.87135
35 – 39	0.096080	53993	5188	257156	1257816	23.296	0.84512
40 – 44	0.113887	48805	5558	230299	1000661	20.503	0.81677
45 – 49	0.137707	43247	5955	201568	770361	17.813	0.78384
50 – 54	0.170740	37292	6367	170579	568793	15.253	0.74068
55 – 59	0.227000	30924	7020	136829	398214	12.877	0.67882
60 – 64	0.274121	23905	6553	102759	261385	10.934	0.60241
65 – 69	0.337299	17352	5853	71604	158626	9.142	0.52331
70 – 74	0.410437	11499	4720	45130	87022	7.568	0.43918
75 – 79	0.492649	6779	3340	24151	41892	6.179	0.35125
80 – 84	0.581642	3440	2001	12196	16741	4.867	0.27024
85 +	1.000000	1439	1439	4544	4544	3.158	0.18067

Source : K.L. Kohli, *Mortality in India*, 1977, pp. 230-231.

Values of SRs are derived from the Lxs.

4

DECADEWISE BIRTHS

Data Required

To estimate the survivors in the 0-4 and 5-9 age groups of a population in a particular census, the total number of births in the last five years and the first five years of the preceding decade are required, as the last five years' births and the first five-years' births of the preceding decade become the cohort population of 0-4 and 5-9 age groups respectively for the succeeding census. For instance the births of 1956-61 (last five years of 1951-61 decade) and 1951-56 (first five years of 1951-61 decade) become the cohort for the age groups 0-4 and 5-9 respectively for the decade 1961-71. The population of the age groups 0-4 and 5-9 of the preceding decade becomes the survivors in the succeeding decade after being exposed to mortality rate in the respective age groups. Therefore, the number of births taking place in a particular decade is required to estimate the population of age groups 0-4 and 5-9 in the subsequent decades.

Data available

The census birth rates for decades 1951-61 and 1961-71 and the year-wise SRS birth rate from 1971 to 1991 are available.

Total population for the census years 1951, 1961, 1971 and 1991 (there was no census in 1981) are available. From these available data on births and population during the period 1951-91, the number of births for the last 5 years, (for 0-4 age group) and for the first 5 years (for 5-9 age group) are estimated as follows :

Decade 1951-61

Total Births for the periods 1951-56 and 1956-61

Step 1 : First, the year-wise population estimates of the decade (1951-1961) are required. For this purpose, the population of 1951 and 1961 censuses are summed up and divided by 2 to arrive at the population for 1956. By dividing the sum of the population of 1951 and 1956 by 2 we get the population for the year 1953.5 which is taken as the population of 1954. The mean of population of the year 1956 and 1954 is taken as the population of 1955; the mean of 1955 and 1951 is taken as the population for 1953, and the mean of 1953 and 1951 population is taken as the population for 1952. This method is followed for estimating year-wise population of the subsequent periods also (Table 4.1).

Step 2 : The year-wise population so estimated is multiplied by the census birth rate of the decade 1951-61 so as to get the total number of births in each year.

Step 3 : The 5-year total of births of the decade are shown in column F of Table 4.1 (Nine- month births for the year 1951 and 3 month births for the year 1956 have to be taken to arrive at 5-year total of births). The same procedure is followed for the second period of the decade also.

Step 4 : These quinquennial births (column F) have been so adjusted as to yield a birth rate very close to the birth rate of 45.4 (Census differencing method). It is to be mentioned that there is no birth rate by Census difference method for the decade 1951-61. But these are 46.7 and 44.1 for the decades 1941-57 and 1961-71 respectively. Therefore average of these two birth rates i.e. (46.7 + 44.1) / 2 = 45.4 is taken as Census differencing birth rate for the decade 1957-67. However survival ratio method yield a birth rate of 49.3 for the decade 1957-61.

Decade 1961-71

Total Births for the periods 1961-66 and 1966-71

Step 1 : The birth rate for the first year of the decade 1961-71 is assumed to be 45.4 (as last year birth rate of 1951-61 decade). But the SRS birth rate stands at 38.5 for the year 1971. To estimate the yearly birth rate for the decade census birth rate of 44.1 is taken as the birth rate for 1966; the mean of birth rates 1961 and 1966 is taken as the birth rate for 1964, the mean of 1964 and 1966 is taken as the birth rate for 1965, the mean of 1961 and 1965 is the birth rate of 1963; the mean of 1963

Table 4.1 : Yearwise Population, Birth Rate and Birth 1951-61

Year	*Population*	*BR*	*Birth*	*Total*	*5yr Total*	*Adjusted*
	A	*B*	*C*	*D*	*E*	*F*
1951	8028856	0.0454	364510	273383	1954217	1985536
1952	8292142	0.0454	376463	376463		
1953	8559427	0.0454	388598	388598		
1954	8730950	0.0454	396385	396385		
1955	9081997	0.0454	412323	412323		
1956	9433043	0.0454	428260	107065		
1956	9433043	0.0454	428260	321195	2260832	2297065
1957	9608567	0.0454	436229	436229		
1958	9784090	0.0454	444198	444198		
1959	10135137	0.0454	460135	460135		
1960	10486183	0.0454	476073	476073		
1961	10837229	0.0454	492010	123003		
Total					4215049	4282601

Adjustment is made from census birth rate

and 1961 as the birth rate for 1962. The same procedure is followed for estimating the yearly birth rate for the second part of the decade.

The total of births for the first 5-year and the second 5-year of the decade are worked out by the method followed for the earlier decade (Step 1 to 3) and these quinquennial births (Column of F) Table 4.2 have been adjusted so as to yield a birth rate which is very closer to 44.1, the birth rate given by 1961-71 Census (census difference method) Table 4.2.

Decade 1971-91

Total Births for the periods 1971-76, 1976-81, 1981-86 and 1986-91

The total number of births for the above quinquennial periods are estimated as follows:

Step 1 : Year-wise mid census year populations are estimated for all the years of the decades 1971-81 and 1981-91. It is to be mentioned that there was no census in 1981, but we have the census interpolated population estimated by the census authority. From this population figure of 1981 year-wise mid-year populations are worked out for the years 1971 to 1991. (By following the procedure explained in Step -1 for the decade 1951-61).

Step 2 : The SRS has provided year-wise and three-year moving average birth rates since 1971 for Assam. In view of the high fluctuations and irregularities of these birth rates another set of birth rates since 1971 is worked out by applying the mid-year birth rate method, where birth rates of 1971, 1981 and 1991 are assumed to be fixed and birth rates for other years are estimated by averaging the initial birth rates of the terminal years of a decade (by applying the same procedure explained in Step 1 of 1961-71 decade).

The total number of births for the periods 1971-76, 1976-81, 1981-86 and 1986-91 are worked out by multiplying the year-wise population and year-wise birth rates. As there are three birth rates – year-wise, three-year moving average and mid-year birth rate), therefore it gives three estimates of total number of births. (Table 4.3).

Out of these three estimates of total number of births (i.e. the sum of the product of year-wise population and year-wise birth rate), for the period 1971-91, such a total number of births is to be selected which gives a birth rate close to 33.54, the SRS average birth rate for the period

Table 4.2 : Yearwise Population, Birth Rate and Birth 1961-71

Year	*Population*	*BR*	*Birth*	*Total*	*5yr Total*	*Adjusted*
	A	*B*	*C*	*D*	*E*	*F*
1961	10837229	0.04540	492010	369008	2589500	2695448
1962	11073975	0.04516	500101	500101		
1963	11310720	0.04492	508078	508078		
1964	11784210	0.04475	527343	527343		
1965	12257700	0.04443	544610	544610		
1966	12731191	0.04410	561446	140361		
1966	12731191	0.04410	561446	421084	2804277	2919012
1967	12967937	0.04305	558270	558270		
1968	13204682	0.04200	554597	554597		
1969	13678172	0.04130	564909	564909		
1970	14151662	0.03990	564651	564651		
1971	14625152	0.03850	563068	140767		
Total					5393778	5614460

Adjustment is made from census birth rate

Table 4.3 : Yearwise Population, Birth rate and Birth 1971-91

YEAR	Population	Y.W.BR	M.A.BR	M.Y. B.R.	Pop x BR	Pop x M.A.	Pop.My BR.	AV	AV Gen	AV1	AV2	AV3
1971	14625152	0.03850	0.03600	0.03850	563068	526505	563068	550881	413161	422301	394879	422301
1972	14945411	0.03640	0.03420	0.03799	544013	511133	567776	540974	540974	544013	511133	567776
1973	15265670	0.03330	0.03200	0.03747	508347	488501	572005	522951	522951	508347	488501	572005
1974	15479176	0.03280	0.03190	0.03713	507717	493786	574742	525415	525415	507717	493786	574742
1975	15906188	0.03010	0.03110	0.03644	478776	494682	579621	517693	517693	478776	494682	579621
1976	16333200	0.03280	0.03130	0.03575	535729	511229	583912	543623	135906	133932	127807	145978
Sum									2656100	2595087	2510789	2862423
Adjusted												2834060
1976	16333200	0.03280	0.03130	0.03575	535729	511229	583912	543623	407718	401797	383422	437934
1977	16653459	0.03010	0.03110	0.03524	501269	517923	586868	535353	535353	501269	517923	586868
1978	16973718	0.03080	0.03220	0.03472	522791	546554	589327	552891	552891	522791	546554	589327
1979	17187224	0.03380	0.03290	0.03438	580928	565460	590897	579095	579095	580928	565460	590897
1980	17614236	0.03190	0.03300	0.03369	561894	581270	593424	578863	578863	561894	581270	593424
1981	18041248	0.03300	0.03400	0.03300	595361	613402	595361	601375	150344	148840	153351	148840
Sum									2804262	2717519	2747978	2947290
Adjusted												2918086

Contd...

YEAR	Population	Y.W.BR	M.A.BR	M.Y. B.R.	Pop x BR	Pop x M.A.	Pop.My BR.	AV	AV Gen	AV1	AV2	AV3
1981	18041248	0.03300	0.03400	0.03300	595361	613402	595361	601375	451031	446521	460052	446521
1982	18451224	0.03420	0.03470	0.03281	631032	640257	605385	625558	625558	631032	640257	605385
1983	18861200	0.03470	0.03470	0.03261	654484	654484	615064	641344	641344	654484	654484	615064
1984	19134517	0.03530	0.03470	0.03248	675448	663968	621489	653635	653635	675448	663968	621489
1985	19681151	0.03430	0.03440	0.03222	675063	677032	634127	662074	662074	675063	677032	634127
1986	20227785	0.03470	0.03390	0.03195	701904	685722	646278	677968	169492	175476	171430	161569
Sum									3203134	3258024	3267223	3084155
Adjusted												3053595
1986	20227785	0.03470	0.03390	0.03195	701904	685722	646278	677968	508476	526428	514291	484708
1987	20637761	0.03420	0.03210	0.03176	705811	662472	655455	674580	674580	705811	662472	655455
1988	21047737	0.03290	0.03060	0.03156	692471	644061	664267	666933	666933	692471	644061	664267
1989	21321054	0.02940	0.03000	0.03143	626839	639632	670121	645530	645530	626839	639632	670121
1990	21867688	0.02970	0.03050	0.03117	649470	666964	681616	666017	666017	649470	666964	681616
1991	22414322	0.03090	0.03040	0.03090	692603	681395	692603	688867	172217	173151	170349	173151
Sum									3333752	3374170	3297769	3329317
Adjusted												3296328

Y.W.BR = Year-wise birth rate
M.A. BR = Moving average birth rate
M.W.BR = Mid-year birth rate
AV = Average birth
AV Gen = General average
AV1 = Average birth from year-wise birth rate
AV2 = Average birth from moving average birth rate
AV3 = Average birth from mid-year birth rate
Adjustment is made from SRS average birth rate for the period 1971-91.

1971-91. (The period-wise total number of birth is worked out by applying the same procedure adopted for 1951-61 decade). The estimated total number of births by period and their respective birth rates are given in Table 4.4.

Table 4.4 shows that the trends of birth rates, except the birth rates worked out from mid-year birth rates (BR-3) are very irregular and their total birth rates for the period 1971-91 are not close to the SRS average birth rate of 33.54. The trend of mid-year birth rates (BR-3) is very smooth and its total number of births for the period 1971-91 gives such a birth rate (33.88) which is close to the SRS average birth rate of 33.54 for the period 1971-91. The estimated number of births by mid-year birth rate for the period 1971-76 to 1986-91 are adjusted so as to yield a birth rate of 33.54 which is close to the SRS average birth rate for the period 1971-91.

Sex Specific Births

The sex specific birth rates are not available in the census and in the SRS reports, but the study requires sex specific total number of births. Further, the number of births are to be specified into male and female. One of the methods to find out male and female births from total births is the sex ratio at birth. In a study on sex ratio at birth Visaria points out that "It is nearly constant within the range of 104-107 (i.e. 962 to 935 females per 1000 males) male live births per 100 female live births in absence of any sex selective intervention".[1] Ramchandran and Despande[2] estimate that the range of sex ratio at birth in India for the period 1949-58 lies within 104-108 (i.e. 962 to 926 females per 1000 males). The SRS gives sex ratio at birth for the year 1970 and 1971 as 952 and 916 females per 1000 males respectively. By observing these sex ratios at birth Dey[3] remarks that a larger proportion of boys than girls are born in Assam. On the contrary Ramchandran and Despande – (by analyzing the sex ratio at birth of 26 countries for the period 1915-1944 have pointed out that "owing to higher biological vulnerability of male foetus, 3-27 per cent more male foetal deaths take place over female foetal deaths.[4] The logic behind this observation is that chances of still male still birth are higher than females. This implies that "larger proportion of male live births than female" may not be the case. Finally, by keeping aside all these arguments it has been suggested that the "expected sex ratio at the early childhood ages are not far below the sex ratio at birth".[5] i.e. sex ratio at early childhood (0-4 age group) can be assumed as sex ratio at birth. Therefore the sex ratio of 0-4 age group of smoothened census population is considered to be relevant

Table 4.4 : Estimated Births and Birth Rates 1971-76 to 1986-91

Period	*Annual BR-1*	*3 year moving*	*Mid year*	*Average (AV) BR -2*	*BR-1*	*BR-2 BR -3*	*BR-3*	*AV*	*Adjusted Average*	*Adjusted Average*
1971-76	2595087	2510789	2862423	2658100	33.53	32.44	36.98	34.34	2834060	36.62
1976-81	2717519	2747978	2947290	2804262	31.62	31.98	34.30	32.63	2918086	33.96
1981-86	3258024	3267223	3084155	3203134	34.05	34.15	32.24	33.48	3053595	31.92
1986-91	3374170	3297769	3329317	3333752	31.65	30.93	31.23	31.27	3296328	30.92
1971-91	11944800	11823759	12223185	11999248	33.10	32.77	33.88	33.26	12102069	33.54

Derived from Table 4.3

to find out the male and female birth for each period. The estimated sex ratios of 0-4 age group smoothened census population are as follows (Table 4.5).

Table 4.5 : 0-4 Age-group Sex Ratio, Assam 1951, 1961, 1971 and 1991

Census year	*0-4 Age Group Sex Eatio*
1951	945
1961	997
1971	998
1991	926

It is to be mentioned that Agnihotri[6] in a study in as many as 364 districts of India finds out a sex ratio of age group 0-4 in between 897 – 1017. This indicates that sex rates at birth may vary between 897 and 1017. Therefore by applying the sex ratio of 0-4 age group smoothened census population the total number of male and female births are estimated and these are presented by Table 4.6.

Table 4.6 : Sex Specific Total Birth 1951-56 to 1986-91

Periods	*Male*	*Female*	*Total*	*Total Birth Rate*
1951-56	1020841	964695	1985516	45.45
1956-61	1181010	1116055	2297065	45.32
1961-66	1349749	1345699	2695448	45.75
1966-71	1461699	1457313	2919012	42.68
1971-76	1418448	1415612	2834060	36.82
1976-81	1460504	1457582	2918086	33.96
1981-86	1585460	1468135	3053595	31.92
1986-91	1711489	1584839	3296328	30.92

References

1. P. Visaria 'The Sex Ratio of the Population of India' Monograph Number 10, Census of India, 1961, New Delhi, R.G. India, in Agnihotri S.B., *Sex Ratio Patterns in the Indian Population*, Sage Publication, New Delhi 2000, p. 62
2. Ramchandran, K.V. and Despande, V.A. "The Sex Ratio at Birth in India by Region", *Milbank Memorial Fund, Quarterly*, 1964, 84-94
3. Quoted from *Census of India,* 1971, Assam General Report, *op cit*, p. 20
4. K.S. Dey, *Census of India*, 1971 Assam, General Report, *op cit.*, p. 20
5. Ramchandran and Despande, *The Sex Ratio at Birth in India by Region*, p.90
6. H.S. Shyrock, *et al. (ed.), Methcds and Materials of Demography, op cit.*, p. 126
7. S.B. Agnihotri, *Sex Ratio Patterns in the Indian Populations*, Sage Publication, New Delhi, 2000, p. 136.

5

Survivors in the age groups 0-4 and 5-9 for the Census years 1961 and 1971 and age groups 0-4 to 15-19 for the Census year 1991

It has already been mentioned that life table survival ratio may be employed for projecting survivors from the age groups 10-14 onwards for the Census population of 1961 and 1971 and age groups 20-24 onwards for the Census population of 1991. Survivors in the age groups below 10-14 for the census years 1961 and 1971, and in the age groups below 20-24 for the Census year 1991 are to be worked out. The method is explained below -

In life table, L_0 represents number of person-years lived during infancy, l_0 represents number of births in the life table cohort. It assumes that –

$$\frac{Po}{B} = \frac{Lo}{lo} \quad \text{....... (1)}$$

Where Po and B are the number of infants at a particular moment, and number of births during preceding 12 months respectively. The estimated number of infant – survivors (Po) and survival ratio (So) of infant can be expressed as follows.[1]

$$Po = \frac{B\,(Lo)}{lo} \quad \text{........ (2)}$$

$$So = \frac{Lo}{lo} \quad \text{........ (3)}$$

In the life table lo is generally assumed to be 100000. If the survival ratio from birth to a given age interval is required, then the form of survival ratio will be as follows.[2]

$$So\text{-}x = \frac{nLx}{nlx} \qquad \text{...... (4)}$$

If the survival ratios from birth to age groups 0-4, 5-9, 10-14, and 15-19 are required, then these can be expressed as follows[3] –

$$S_{0\text{-}4} = \frac{L_{0\text{-}4}}{5l_0} \qquad \text{...... (5)}$$

$$S_{5\text{-}4} = \frac{L_{5\text{-}9}}{5l_0} \qquad \text{...... (6)}$$

$$S_{10\text{-}14} = \frac{L_{10\text{-}14}}{5l_0} \qquad \text{...... (7)}$$

$$S_{15\text{-}19} = \frac{L_{15\text{-}19}}{5l_0} \qquad \text{...... (8)}$$

Where $L_{0\text{-}4}$, $L_{5\text{-}9}$, $L_{10\text{-}14}$, and $L_{15\text{-}19}$ are the number of person-years lived in the age groups 0-4, 5-9, 10-14 and 15-19 respectively.

The equation 2 above gives the number of infant survivors at a point of time as –

$$P_0 = B\frac{(L_0)}{l_0} \quad \text{where} \quad \frac{(L_0)}{l_0} \text{ is the survival ratio.}$$

By following the equations 1 and 2 the number of survivors in an age group can be worked out from the relations of life table function as follows –

$$\frac{Pxt}{B5yt} = \frac{Lx}{5l_0}$$

$$Pxt = B5yt \frac{Lx}{5l_0} \qquad \text{...... (9)}$$

where Pxt is the number of survivors in the age group x at a point of time t, B5yt is the number of births during the preceding 5 years of time t and $Lx/5l_0$ is the survival ratio of age group x. Thus the number of survivors in the age groups 0-4, 5-9, 10-14 and 15-19 can be worked out by applying the equation 9.

$$P_{0-4} = B5yt \frac{L_{0-4}}{5l_0} \qquad \text{...... (10)}$$

$$P_{5-4} = B5yt \frac{L_{5-9}}{5l_0} \qquad \text{...... (11)}$$

$$P_{10-14} = B5yt \frac{L_{10-14}}{5l_0} \qquad \text{...... (12)}$$

$$P_{15-19} = B5yt \frac{L_{15-19}}{5l_0} \qquad \text{...... (13)}$$

By applying equation 10 and 11, the number of survivors in the age groups 0-4 and 5-9 for the decades 1951-61 and 1961-71 (more specifically for the Census years 1961 and 1971) are worked out. For doing so, the number of survivors in these two age groups, the number of births by sex of the periods 1951-56, 1956-61, 1961-66 and 1966-71 are taken from Table 4 of Chapter IV and those of survival ratios by sex in the respective age groups are worked out from life tables of 1951-61 and 1961-71 decades.

The survival ratio of the age groups 0-4 and 5-9 for the census year 1991 cannot be worked out from 1971-91 Life table, because the children born during 1986-91 and 1981-86 become the survivors in the age groups 0-4 and 5-9 respectively. Therefore, to work out the survival ratios for these age groups, the life table for the decade 1981-91 has to be used. In the same way, the survival ratio of the age groups 10-14 and 15-19 for the period 1971-91 are worked out from the life table of 1971-81 decade,

Table 5.1 : Survivors in the Age Groups 0-4 and 5-9 for decades 1951-61 and 1961-71 and the age groups 0-4 to 15-19 for the period 1971-91

	Male				Female			
Period	*Birth*	*Survival Ratio*	*Age group*	*Survivor*	*Birth*	*Survival Ratio*	*Age group*	*Survivor*
1956-61	1181010	0.74867	0-4	884182	1116055	0.798874	0-4	891587
1951-56	1020641	0.67180	5-9	685865	964695	0.729154	5-9	703411

	Male				Female			
Period	*Birth*	*Survival Ratio*	*Age group*	*Survivor*	*Birth*	*Survival Ratio*	*Age group*	*Survivor*
1966-71	1428947	0.805242	0-4	1150648	1424661	0.809028	0-4	1152591
1961-66	1382500	0.741388	5-9	1024969	1378352	0.740666	5-9	1020898

	Male				Female			
Period	*Birth*	*Survival Ratio*	*Age group*	*Survivor*	*Birth*	*Survival Ratio*	*Age group*	*Survivor*
1986-91	1711489	0.86759	0-4	1484871	1584839	0.86933	0-4	1377748
1981-86	1585460	0.82238	5-9	1303851	1468135	0.81734	5-9	1199965
1976-81	1460504	0.77723	10-14	1135148	145782	0.77472	10-14	1129218
1971-76	1418448	0.767182	15-19	1088208	1415612	0.76372	15-19	1081131

Note :
1. Survival Ratios for the period 1951-56 and 1956-61 are derived from life table 1951-61
2. Survival Ratios for the period 1961-66 and 1966-71 are derived from life table 1961-71
3. Survival Ratios for the period 1971-76 and 1976-81 are derived from life table 1971-81
4. Survival Ratios for the period 1981-86 and 1986-91 are derived from life table 1981-91.

as the survivors in 10-14 and 15-19 age groups in 1991 Census were born in the decade 1971-81. By applying these survival ratios the age groups 0-4, 5-9, 10-14 and 15-19 for the period 1971-91, the number of survivors in these age groups are worked out. Table 5.1 gives the number of births, survivors and survival ratios for the periods 1951-56 to 1986-91.

The estimates of survivors in the age groups in different census years mentioned in Table 5.1, have been arrived at by the application of forward survival ratio method, i.e. by taking the survivor in each age group as the product of births and their respective survival ratio. Similarly by applying the reverse survival ratio method i.e., the ratio between 5-year age group smoothened census population of the succeeding census and the survival ratio of the respective age groups, the number of survivors in the respective age groups can also be worked out. This is shown in Chapter VI.

References

1. G.W. Barclay, *Technique of Population Analysis*, John Willey and Sons, New York, 1966, p. 129.
2. H.S. Shryock, *et al.* (ed) *Methods and Materials of Demography*, *op cit*, p. 263
3. *ibid*, p. 358

6

Estimating Migration

This chapter is devoted to estimating migration by applying the methods discussed in Chapter 1.

Direct Method

As mentioned earlier, census birth place statistics provide the only direct method of estimating migration. Table 6.1 gives the volume of migration to Assam based on place of birth in the Census years 1951, 1961, 1971 and 1991. (Tables 6.2, to 6.7 give the district-wise migration to Assam based on place of birth data.)

It has already been mentioned in Chapter 1 that there are gross inaccuracies in the census place of birth statistics, as a result of which the estimates of migration based on this method are not at all reliable . That the estimates of migrants based on census place of birth data are not reliable becomes evident if we compare the figures of migrants given in 1991 Census report (in migration table) with figures given in the migration table of 1971 Census report. Table 6.1 shows that the number of migrants (based on census place of birth statistics) had declined from 1465231 in 1971 to 876134 in 1991. This implies out-migration of a percentage of the pre-1971 migrants from Assam during 1971-91. Alternatively, some migrant had reported their place of birth incorrectly . strangely in the same census report, the migration table shows that during the period 1971-91 more than 3 lakh persons migrated to Assam. This contradiction in the census report gives an indication of the unreliability of place of birth statistics.

Table 6.1 : Interstate and International Migration to Assam : 1951-1991 Estimate Based on Place Birth Data (Estimate – 1)

Year	*Interstate*			*International*			*Total*		
	Migrants	*(+) (-)*	*(%)(±)*	*Migrants*	*(+) (-)*	*(%)(±)*	*Migrants*	*(+) (-)*	*(%)(±)*
1951	449646	-		866268	-		1315954	-	
1961	468062	18416	4.09	813346	-52922	-6.11	1281408	-34546	-2.63
1971	505425	40363	7.98	959826	146480	18.01	1465251	183843	+14.35
1991	536579	31154	6.16	339555	-620271	-64.62	876134	-589117	-40.21

Source : *Census of India* 1951, 1961, 1971 and 1991, Assam, Migration Tables

Note : The migration figures are adjusted for the present political boundary of Assam.

Table 6.2 : District-wise Interstate and International Migration to Assam : 1951 Census (Based on Census Place of Birth Statistics)

District	*Interstate*			*International*		
	Total	*Male*	*Female*	*Total*	*Male*	*Female*
1. Goalpara	36370	23569	12801	140164	80778	59386
2. Kamrup	29240	21333	7907	193527	110535	82992
3. Darrang	98856	54819	44037	95227	50390	44837
4. Nagaon	29079	18747	10332	174929	99199	75730
5. Lakhimpur	146809	84485	62324	75549	43448	32101
6. Sibsagar	73788	43638	30150	30342	17673	12669
7. Cachar	24466	15344	9122	130281	70499	59782
8. N.C. Hills	11078	8584	2494	26249	16159	10090
Assam	449686	270519	179167	866268	488681	377587

Table 6.3 : District-wise Interstate and International Migration to Assam : 1961 Census (Based on Census Place of Birth Statistics)

District	*Interstate*			*International*		
	Total	*Male*	*Female*	*Total*	*Male*	*Female*
1. Goalpara	50672	34157	16515	150164	82199	67965
2. Kamrup	50632	38428	12204	144852	82760	62092
3. Darrang	91256	58290	32966	108060	62868	45192
4. Nagaon	42964	33941	9023	140078	79535	60543
5. Lakhimpur	140435	97690	42745	91291	57521	33770
6. Sibsagar	63016	42711	20305	26482	17276	9206
7. Cachar	21534	13215	8319	134773	70543	64230
8. N.C. Hills	7553	5259	2294	17646	11272	6374
Assam	468062	323691	144371	813346	463974	349372

Table 6.4 : District-wise Interstate and International Migration to Assam : 1971 Census (Based on Census Place of Birth Statistics)

District	*Interstate*			*International*		
	Total	*Male*	*Female*	*Total*	*Male*	*Female*
1. Goalpara	70764	44226	26538	183226	98401	84825
2. Kamrup	77645	52902	24743	179565	99181	80384
3. Darrang	89062	58332	30730	112268	62673	49595
4. Nagaon	42982	29061	13921	180379	93424	86955
5. Lakhimpur	130470	94309	36161	116324	63753	52571
6. Sibsagar	67412	46817	20595	36882	23571	13311
7. Cachar	24270	16175	8095	146826	76567	70259
8. N.C. Hills	2820	1880	940	4356	2700	1656
Assam	505425	343702	161723	959826	520270	439556

Source of Tables 6.2, 6.3 and 6.4 : *Censuses of India* : 1951, 1961, 1971 Assam,

Migration Tables.

Table 6.5 : District-wise Interstate and International Migration to Assam : 1991 Census (Based on Census Place of Birth Statistics)

District	0-9 Years' duration						10-19 Years' duration					
	Interstate			International			Interstate			International		
	Total	Male	Female	Total	Male	Female	Total	Male	Female	Total	Male	Female
1. Dhubri	8180	2380	5800	570	320	250	6180	1810	4370	603	260	343
2. Kokrajhar	5290	1890	3400	760	320	440	5622	2420	3202	1040	440	600
3. Bongaigaon	6480	3240	3240	970	500	470	6100	3050	3050	1350	640	710
4. Goalpara	2762	1560	1202	420	280	140	1930	930	1000	570	250	320
5. Barpeta	3330	1930	1400	1130	670	460	1960	1040	920	1310	590	720
6. Nalbari	2950	1760	1190	520	330	190	2757	1327	1430	590	260	330
7. Kamrup	35300	20800	14500	2310	1180	1130	22395	13250	9145	2390	1330	1060
8. Darrang	4710	2720	1990	685	345	340	6210	3170	3040	1340	690	650
9. Sonitpur	13190	7358	5832	630	320	310	7850	4140	3710	930	410	520
10. Lakhimpur	3700	2570	1130	340	170	170	2802	1782	1020	550	260	290
11. Dhemaji	3855	2365	1490	370	210	160	2157	1167	990	590	340	250
12. Marigaon	2500	1410	1090	280	160	120	1020	570	450	210	90	120
13. Nagaon	7890	4490	3400	1410	790	620	5860	2880	2980	1900	660	1240
14. Golaghat	5550	3860	1690	190	100	90	3690	2140	1550	183	83	100
15. Jorhat	6059	4100	1959	290	190	100	3954	2334	1620	280	120	160

Contd...

District	0-9 Years' duration						10-19 Years' duration					
	Interstate			International			Interstate			International		
	Total	Male	Female	Total	Male	Female	Total	Male	Female	Total	Male	Female
16. Sibsagar	7100	5140	1960	160	110	50	3410	2240	1170	170	120	50
17. Dibrugarh	11689	7415	4274	340	210	130	8256	5000	3256	290	130	160
18. Tinsukia	11920	7420	4500	800	410	390	11121	6751	4370	920	510	410
19. K. Anglong	7458	4376	3082	460	270	190	6113	3581	2532	870	450	420
20. N.C. Hills	2570	1680	890	300	250	50	1420	770	650	260	180	80
21. Karimganj	4930	1950	2980	1002	569	433	4327	1697	2630	1450	630	820
22. Hailakandi	2840	1530	1310	280	180	100	1220	530	690	420	170	250
23. Cachar	9310	5200	4110	4170	2030	2140	4708	2000	2708	4200	1960	2240
Assam	169563	97144	72419	18387	9914	8473	121062	64579	56483	22416	10573	11843

Source : *Census of India* : 1991 Assam, Migration Tables

Table 6.6 : Interstate and International Migration to Assam : 1991 Census (Based on Census Place of Birth Statistics)

District	0-19 Years' duration						Place of Birth (All duration)					
	Interstate			International			Interstate			International		
	Total	Male	Female	Total	Male	Female	Total	Male	Female	Total	Male	Female
1. Dhubri	14360	4190	10170	1173	580	593	24373	8710	15663	14292	7410	6882
2. Kokrajhar	10912	4310	6602	1800	760	1040	19578	9046	10532	13314	7450	5864
3. Bongaigaon	12580	6290	6290	2320	1140	1180	21490	11430	10060	22765	12540	10225
4. Goalpara	4692	2490	2202	990	530	460	8452	4850	3602	12311	6721	5590
5. Barpcta	5290	2970	2320	2440	1260	1180	8631	4820	3811	21450	11100	10350
6. Nalbari	5707	3087	2620	1110	590	520	10297	6037	4260	9860	5370	4490
7. Kamrup	57695	34050	23645	4700	2510	2190	93714	57056	36658	27852	15402	12450
8. Darrang	10920	5890	5030	2025	1035	990	25990	14720	11270	19927	11092	8835
9. Sonitpur	21040	11498	9542	1560	730	830	40900	23048	17852	18120	10060	8060
10. Lakhimpur	6502	4352	2150	890	430	460	11376	7536	3840	6070	3410	2660
11. Dhemaji	6012	3532	2480	960	550	410	10317	6567	3750	7133	4130	3003
12. Marigaon	3520	1980	1540	490	250	240	5980	3530	2450	7780	4320	3460
13. Nagaon	13750	7370	6380	3310	1450	1860	30400	17330	13070	48481	26687	21794
14. Golaghat	9240	6000	3240	373	183	190	18540	11190	7350	2803	1583	1220
15. Jorhat	10013	6434	3579	570	310	260	18435	12256	6179	2392	1452	940

Contd...

District	0-19 Years' duration						Place of Birth (All duration)					
	Interstate			International			Interstate			International		
	Total	Male	Female	Total	Male	Female	Total	Male	Female	Total	Male	Female
16. Sibsagar	10510	7380	3130	330	230	100	17051	11430	5621	1960	1190	770
17. Dibrugarh	19945	12415	7530	630	340	290	41014	25422	15592	6790	3900	2890
18. Tinsukia	23041	14171	8870	1720	920	800	52456	32626	19830	11880	6840	5040
19. K. Anglong	13571	7957	5614	1330	720	610	31391	18327	13064	10400	6010	4390
20. N.C. Hills	3990	2450	1540	560	430	130	6090	3690	2400	2010	1380	630
21. Karimganj	9257	3647	5610	2452	1199	1253	14615	5870	8745	29428	15245	14183
22. Hailakandi	4060	2060	2000	700	350	350	6150	3150	3000	6326	3266	3060
23. Cachar	14018	7200	6818	8370	3990	4380	19339	9761	9578	36211	18580	17631
Assam	290625	161723	128902	40803	20487	20316	536579	308402	228177	339555	185138	154417

Source : *Census of India* : 1991 Assam, Migration Tables V- I

Table 6.7 : Interstate and International Migration to Assam : 1991 Census (Based on Census Place of Birth Statistics)

District	Less than 1 Year duration						1-4 Years' duration					
	Interstate			International			Interstate			International		
	Total	Male	Female	Total	Male	Female	Total	Male	Female	Total	Male	Female
1. Dhubri	760	350	410	100	60	40	3780	1160	2620	270	160	110
2. Kokrajhar	390	160	230	50	20	30	2140	670	1470	400	180	220
3. Bongaigaon	780	600	180	120	90	30	2810	1390	1420	370	170	200
4. Goalpara	340	220	120	90	60	30	1300	730	570	150	90	60
5. Barpeta	750	680	70	150	110	40	1380	740	640	480	280	200
6. Nalbari	600	460	140	80	80	0	1150	680	470	210	130	80
7. Kamrup	4620	3210	1410	300	140	160	17294	9804	7490	980	500	480
8. Darrang	700	580	120	70	30	40	1990	1110	880	230	140	90
9. Sonitpur	1921	1149	772	40	40	0	6499	3699	2800	260	90	170
10. Lakhimpur	620	520	100	50	20	30	1780	1260	520	150	90	60
11. Dhemaji	545	415	130	20	10	10	1990	1210	780	120	60	60
12. Marigaon	490	380	110	20	10	10	770	390	380	160	80	80
13. Nagaon	1070	800	270	380	280	100	3500	1960	1540	530	240	290
14. Golaghat	850	690	160	0	0	0	2510	1770	740	120	70	50
15. Jorhat	1000	820	180	50	50	0	2749	1810	939	120	70	50

Contd...

District	Less than 1 Year duration						1-4 Years' duration					
	Interstate			International			Interstate			International		
	Total	Male	Female	Total	Male	Female	Total	Male	Female	Total	Male	Female
16. Sibsagar	1044	854	190	0	0	0	3640	2590	1050	90	60	30
17. Dibrugarh	1581	1151	430	40	40	0	5150	3300	1850	140	90	50
18. Tinsukia	1300	980	320	110	50	60	5040	3120	1920	320	140	180
19. K. Anglong	770	460	310	100	60	40	3388	1916	1472	150	80	70
20. N.C. Hills	550	480	70	10	10	0	1140	730	410	140	110	30
21. Karimganj	580	340	240	79	59	20	2120	830	1290	400	240	160
22. Hailakandi	280	150	130	40	30	10	1700	990	710	130	80	50
23. Cachar	1290	930	360	330	220	110	4480	2530	1950	1930	970	960
Assam	22831	16379	6452	2229	1469	760	78300	44389	33911	7850	4120	3730

Source : *Census of India*, 1991 Assam, Migration Tables

Indirect Methods

1. Residual or Vital Statistics Method

It has been already explained in Chapter 1 that migration (in or out) in Census year X is equal to difference between the population of census year X and the sum of the population of the preceding census year X-1 and difference of births and deaths between the census years X and X-1. Tables 2.8 and 2.9 give the decade-wise vital statistics and total difference between births and deaths respectively. Table 2.10 gives the decade-wise estimates of migrants to Assam based on vital statistics.

Table 6.8 : Decade-wise Birth and Death Rates : Assam : 1951-61 to 1981-91

Decade	*Birth Rate*	*Death Rate*	*Natural growth rate*
1951-61	45.4	26.9	20.5
1961-71	44.1	19.6	24.5
1971-81	33.05	14.89	18.16
1981-91	33.15	13.47	19.68

Source : (i) *Census of India* 1961, 1971
(ii) SRS *Compendium of India's Fertility and Mortality Indicators*, the Registrar General, India, 1997

Table 6.9 : Total Births, Deaths and their Difference : Assam : 1951-61 to 1981-91

Decade	*Mid year population*	*Total Births*	*Total Deaths*	*Difference*
1951-61	9433043	4282610	2537489	1745121
1961-71	12731191	5614460	2495313	3119147
1971-81	16333200	5398123	2432013	2966109
1981-91	20227785	6705511	2966109	3980828

Table 6.10 : (Estimate 2) Decade-wise Migration to Assam : 1951-61 to 1981-91 (Estimates by Vital Statistics Method)

Decade	P_0	P_1	$B-D$	M
1951-61	8028856	10837329	1745121	1063352
1961-71	10837329	14625152	3119147	668776
1971-81	14625152	18041248	2966109	449987
1981-91	18041248	22414322	3980828	392246

Survival Method

The method of estimating migration by survival method has been discussed in Chapter I. The data required for estimating migration by this method are worked out in Chapters II to V. It has already been mentioned that survival ratio method can be directly used to estimate the survivors and migration for the age groups 10-14 onwards for the decades 1951-61 and 1961-71 and age groups 20-24 onwards for the period 1971-91. To estimate survivors in the age groups below 10-14 for the decades 1951-61 and 1961-71 and below 20-24 for the period 1971-91, both the forward and reverse survival ratio methods have been used. These are explained in Chapters V and VI. By applying the survival ratios (Chapter III) migrants by age and sex are estimated for the decades 1951-61, 1961-71 and for the period 1971-91. By applying the survival ratio methods migrants by age and sex are estimated for the decades 1951-61, 1961-71 and for the period 1971-91 (Tables 6.11 to 6.16).

Both the indirect methods (viz. method 1 and 2) give almost the similar estimates of migrants to Assam during different periods, viz, 1951-61, 1961-71, 1971-91. Between these two indirect methods, vital statistics method and survival ratio method, the latter is considered to be more accurate because the estimates of migration based on vital statistics method are more likely to be erroneous as under this method "relatively moderate errors in population counts or in statistics of births and deaths produce much larger percentage errors in the migration estimates".[1] In contrast the estimates of migration based on average of reverse and forward survival rates method are free from such possibilities as the total population is split into different age groups and their corresponding survival ratios are used instead of the single births or deaths figure for the entire population.

Noteworthy, that the estimate of immigrants coming from various countries to the USA during 1950-60, by using the survival method, were found to be very close to the actual figures found in the visa and other official statistics.[2]

Thus the net migration to Assam during 1951-61, 1961-71, and 1971-91 stood at 1067846, 801880 and 976969 respectively, according to this study.

Composition of Migrants : Inter-state and International

The place of birth data of the persons enumerated are available in

Table 6.11 : Age Specific Migration to Assam by Survival Ratio Method : Male : 1951-61

	1951				1961				
Age-group	*Pop.*	*SR*	*Pop.Forward*	*Age-group*	*Pop.*	*Mign-1*	*Pop.Reverse*	*Mign-2*	*M1+M2/2*
Birth 1956-61	1181010	0.74867	884182	0-4	923838	39656	1233979	52969	46312
Birth 1951-56	1020641	0.67180	685665	5 to 9	782510	96845	1164800	144159	120502
0-4	695812	0.86653	602942	10 to 14	681432	78490	786392	90580	84535
5 to 9	585239	0.94518	553156	15 to 19	608651	55495	643952	58713	57104
10 to 14	484160	0.95408	461927	20 to 24	537844	75917	563731	79571	77744
15 to 19	407289	0.94406	384505	25 to 29	467037	82532	494711	87422	84977
20 to 24	350782	0.92895	325859	30 to 34	396230	70371	426535	75753	73062
25 to 29	311814	0.90759	282999	35 to 39	325423	42424	358557	46743	44584
30 to 34	285318	0.87931	250883	40 to 44	267925	17042	304699	19381	18212
35 to 39	258784	0.84310	218181	45 to 49	227381	9200	269696	10912	10056
40 to 44	226721	0.79443	180114	50 to 54	188594	8480	237395	10674	9577
45 to 49	190150	0.72495	137849	55 to 59	145666	7817	200932	10782	9300
50 to 54	151069	0.63638	96137	60 to 64	103539	7402	162700	11631	9516
55 to 59	115351	0.53652	61888	65 to 69	65742	3854	122534	7183	5518
60 to 64	89915	0.42592	38297	70 to 74	40093	1796	94133	4218	3007
65 to 69	68051	0.31115	21174	75 to 79	22462	1288	72190	4139	2714
70 to 74	49127	0.21177	10404	80 to 84	10404		49127		
75+	29191	0.12350	3605	85+	3605		29191		
Total	4298773		5199768		5798376	598608		714831	656720

Table 6.12 : Age Specific Migration to Assam by Survival Ratio Method : Female : 1951-61

	1951			*1961*					
Age-group	*Pop.*	*SR*	*Pop.Forward*	*Age-group*	*Pop.*	*Mign-1*	*Pop.Reverse*	*Mign-2*	*M1+M2/2*
Birth 1956-61	1116055	0.79887	891587	0-4	921101	29514	1152999	36944	33229
Birth 1951-56	964695	0.72915	703411	5 to 9	740146	36735	1015075	50380	43557
0-4	657974	0.87829	577892	10 to 14	624762	46870	711339	53365	50118
5 to 9	549758	0.93061	511610	15 to 19	543509	31899	584035	34277	33088
10 to 14	441538	0.92238	407266	20 to 24	462565	55299	501491	59953	57626
15 to 19	361845	0.89685	324521	25 to 29	381621	57100	425513	63668	60384
20 to 24	300330	0.87135	261693	30 to 34	300677	38984	345070	44740	41862
25 to 29	257816	0.84512	217885	35 to 39	246973	29088	292234	34418	31753
30 to 34	230852	0.81677	188553	40 to 44	205718	17165	251868	21016	19090
35 to 39	207333	0.78384	162516	45 to 49	172771	10255	220416	13083	11669
40 to 44	180014	0.74068	133333	50 to 54	139824	6491	188778	8764	7628
45 to 49	149250	0.67882	101314	55 to 59	106877	5563	157445	8195	6879
50 to 54	118486	0.60241	71377	60 to 64	75930	4553	126044	7558	6055
55 to 59	90118	0.52331	47160	65 to 69	50566	3406	96627	6509	4958
60 to 64	69737	0.43918	30627	70 to 74	31369	742	71426	1689	1216
65 to 69	53415	0.35125	18762	75 to 79	19809	1047	56396	2981	2014
70 to 74	38913	0.27024	10516	80 to 84	10516		38913		
75+	23353	0.18067	4219	85+	4219		23353		
Total	3730732		4664242		5038953	374711		447540	411126

Table 6.13 : Age Specific Migration to Assam by Survival Ratio Method : Male : 1961-71

	1961				*1961*				
Age-group	*Pop.*	*SR*	*Pop.Forward*	*Age-group*	*Pop.*	*Mign-1*	*Pop.Reverse*	*Mign-2*	*M1+M2/2*
Birth 1966-71	1461699	0.80524	1177021	0-4	1213550	36529	1507062	45363	40946
Birth 1961-66	1349749	0.74139	1000688	5 to 9	1048138	47450	1413751	64002	55726
0-4	923838	0.89814	829736	10 to 14	882090	52354	982130	58292	55323
5 to 9	782510	0.96145	752344	15 to 19	789861	37517	821531	39021	38269
10 to 14	681432	0.97016	661098	20 to 24	711833	50735	733727	52295	51515
15 to 19	608651	0.9641	586800	25 to 29	630186	43386	653652	45001	44193
20 to 24	537844	0.95531	513808	30 to 34	543414	29606	568835	30991	30299
25 to 29	467037	0.94594	441789	35 to 39	466892	25103	493575	26538	25820
30 to 34	396230	0.92262	365570	40 to 44	385245	19675	417555	21325	20500
35 to 39	325423	0.87667	285289	45 to 49	303598	18309	346308	20885	19597
40 to 44	267925	0.82257	220387	50 to 54	230710	10323	280475	12550	11436
45 to 49	227381	0.77168	175465	55 to 59	182451	6986	236433	9052	8019
50 to 54	188594	0.68612	129398	60 to 64	136615	7217	199112	10518	8868
55 to 59	145666	0.57874	84303	65 to 69	90749	6446	156804	11138	8792
60 to 64	103539	0.46204	47839	70 to 74	53957	6118	116780	13241	9679
65 to 69	65742	0.36793	24188	75 to 79	24188		65742		
70 to 74	40093	0.29163	11692	80 to 84	11692		40093		
75 to 79	22462	0.23078	5183	85 to 89	5183		22462		
80+	14009	0.27751	3888	90 +	3888		14009		
	8609824		7316486		7714240	397754		460214	428984

Table 6.14 : Age Specific Migration to Assam by Survival Ratio Method : Female : 1961-71

	1961						*1961*		
Age-group	*Pop.*	*SR*	*Pop.Forward*	*Age-group*	*Pop.*	*Mign-1*	*Pop.Reverse*	*Mign-2*	*M1+M2/2*
Birth 1966-71	1457313	0.80903	1149112	0-4	1211698	62586	1497721	40408	51497
Birth 1961-66	1345699	0.74067	990336	5 to 9	1044274	53938	1409912	64213	59076
0-4	921101	0.89096	820664	10 to 14	846406	25742	949993	28892	27317
5 to 9	740146	0.95716	708438	15 to 19	725810	17372	758295	18149	17761
10 to 14	624762	0.96133	600602	20 to 24	622028	21426	647049	22287	21856
15 to 19	543509	0.94042	511127	25 to 29	537867	26740	571943	28434	27587
20 to 24	462565	0.91503	423261	30 to 34	453706	30445	495837	33272	31859
25 to 29	381621	0.894	341169	35 to 39	369545	28376	413361	31740	30058
30 to 34	300677	0.87341	262614	40 to 44	292303	29689	334669	33992	31840
35 to 39	246973	0.85328	210737	45 to 49	227153	16416	266212	19239	17827
40 to 44	205718	0.8336	171487	50 to 54	184232	12745	221008	15290	14018
45 to 49	172771	0.7978	137837	55 to 59	146484	8647	183610	10839	9743
50 to 54	139824	0.72215	100974	60 to 64	108209	7235	149843	10019	8627
55 to 59	106877	0.57887	61868	65 to 69	69934	8066	120811	13934	11000
60 to 64	75930	0.41577	31569	70 to 74	39105	7536	94054	18124	12830
65 to 69	50566	0.32205	16284	75 to 79	16284		50566		
70 to 74	31369	0.26401	8282	80 to 84	8282		31369		
75 to 79	19809	0.20722	4105	85 to 89	4105		19809		
80+	14735	0.23664	3487	90 +	3487		14735		
	7841965		6553953		6910912	356959		388833	372896

Table 6.15 : Age Specific Migration to Assam by Survival Ratio Method : Male : 1971-91

	1971			1991					
Age-group	*Pop.*	*SR*	*Pop.Forward*	*Age-group*	*Pop.*	*Mign-1*	*Pop.Reverse*	*Mign-2*	*M1+M2/2*
Birth 1986-91	1711489	0.86759	1484871	0-4	1516538	31667	17474989	36500	34084
Birth 1981-86	1585460	0.82238	1303851	5 to 9	1374147	70296	1670939	85479	77888
Birth 1976-81	1460504	0.77723	1135148	10 to 14	1234790	99642	1588706	i28202	113922
Birth 1971-76	1418448	0.76718	1088208	15 to 19	1157283	69075	1508486	90038	79556
0-4	1213530	0.90226	1094920	20 to 24	1136106	41186	1259178	45648	43417
5 to 9	1048138	0.94227	987629	25 to 29	1015875	28246	1078115	29977	29111
10 to 14	882090	0.94300	831811	30 to 34	873222	41411	926004	43914	42663
15 to 19	789861	0.92973	734357	35 to 39	756135	21778	813285	23424	22601
20 to 24	711833	0.90373	643305	40 to 44	664783	21478	735599	23766	22622
25 to 29	630186	0.86232	543422	45 to 49	563058	19636	652957	22771	21204
30 to 34	543414	0.80044	434971	50 to 54	450386	15415	562672	19258	17336
35 to 39	466982	0.72231	337306	55 to 59	347353	10047	480892	13910	11979
40 to 44	385245	0.62388	240347	60 to 64	248522	8175	398348	13103	10639
45 to 49	303598	0.49354	149837	65 to 69	155117	5280	314295	10697	7988
50 to 54	230710	0.35434	81749	70 to 74	81749		230710		
55 to 59	182451	0.23780	43387	75 to 79	43387		182451		
60 to 64	136615	0.15195	20759	80 to 84	20759		136615		
65 to 69	90749	0.09825	8916	85 to 89	8916		90749		
70+	98908	0.09972	9863	90 +	9863		98908		
	7714310		11174657		11657989	483332		586686	535009

Table 6.16 : Age Specific Migration to Assam by Survival Ratio Method : Female : 1971-91

	1971			1991					
Age-group	*Pop.*	*SR*	*Pop.Forward*	*Age-group*	*Pop.*	*Mign-1*	*Pop.Reverse*	*Mign-2*	*M1+M2/2*
Birth 1986-91	1584839	0.86933	1377748	0-4	1404691	26943	1615832	30993	28968
Birth 1981-86	1468135	0.81734	1199965	5 to 9	1262910	62945	1545146	77011	69978
Birth 1976-81	1457582	0.77472	1129218	10 to 14	1202181	72963	1551762	94180	83571
Birth 1971-76	1415612	0.76372	1081131	15 to 19	1139730	58599	1492340	76727	67664
0-4	1211698	0.88852	1076618	20 to 24	1116086	39468	1256118	44420	41944
5 to 9	1044274	0.91808	958727	25 to 29	1000023	41296	1089255	44981	43138
10 to 14	846406	0.90482	765845	30 to 34	809153	43308	894270	47864	45586
15 to 19	725810	0.88201	640172	35 to 39	660408	20236	748753	22943	21590
20 to 24	622028	0.86475	537899	40 to 44	552366	14467	638758	16730	15599
25 to 29	537867	0.85266	458618	45 to 49	464867	6249	545196	7329	6789
30 to 34	453706	0.82262	373228	50 to 54	377906	4678	459393	5687	5183
35 to 39	369545	0.77124	285008	55 to 59	287531	2523	372817	3272	2897
40 to 44	292303	0.68156	199222	60 to 64	201552	2330	295722	3419	2874
45 to 49	227153	0.54461	123710	65 to 69	126067	2357	237153	10000	6179
50 to 54	184232	0.40140	73951	70 to 74	73951		184232		
55 to 59	146484	0.27412	40154	75 to 79	40154		146484		
60 to 64	108209	0.17932	19404	80 to 84	19404		108209		
65 to 69	69934	0.11846	8284	85 to 89	8284		69934		
70+	71263	0.12726	9069	90 +	9069		71263		
	6910912		10357970		10756333	398363		485556	441960

Tables 6.17 summarises the findings of Tables 6.11 to 6.16. It shows that the total migrants during 1951-1991 stood at 28,46,695.

Table 6.17 : Migration by Survival Method

Decade	*Forward Survival Method*			*Reverse Survival Method*			*Average*		
	Male	*Female*	*Total*	*Male*	*Female*	*Total*	*Male*	*Female*	*Total*
1951-61	598608	374711	973319	714831	447540	1162371	656720	411126	1067846
1961-71	397754	356959	754713	460214	388833	849047	428984	372896	801880
1971-91	483333	398363	881696	586686	485556	1072242	535009	441960	976969
Total	1479695	1130033	2609728	1761731	1321929	3083660	1620713	1225982	2846695

the Census Reports. Persons actually born elsewhere in India and enumerated in Assam are expected to report their place of birth correctly, because every citizen of India has the right to move anywhere within the country (although the possibility of a section of interstate migrants first entering other neighbouring states viz., West Bengal, Bihar, Meghalaya, Tripura etc. subsequently migrating to Assam and reporting the initial place of entry as the place of birth cannot be ruled out). But those foreign migrants who have directly entered Assam illegally would never disclose their actual place of birth to avoid possible punitive actions. Hence, while the census data on internal migration can not be taken as totally accurate, those of international migration are definitely so. Keeping in mind the above, a rough estimate of inter-state and international migrants is made by deducting from the total migrants of each period the number of inter-state migrants as found in the corresponding census reports (Table 6.18). In reality, the number of inter-state migrants is likely to be less and that of international migrants more.

Table 6.18 : Composition of Migrants : Interstate and International

Decade/Period	*Interstate* *A*	*Total estimated migrant* *B*	*International migrant* *(B – A = C)*
1951-61	260636	1067846	807210
1961-71	340476	801880	461404
1971-91	290625	976969	686344
Total	891737	2846695	1954958

Source : For 0-9 years' duration inter-state birth place data : *Census of India* 1961, 1971 and 1991 migration table.

Note : Inter-state birth place data forthe period 1961-71 relate to 0-10 years' duration of stay , as no 0-9 year duration of stay figures are available. This has deflated the volume of international migrants of the decade 1961-71 at least by 340476/10 = 34047. Thus the international migrants during the decade 1961-71 would be 461404 + 34047 = 495461.

Composition of Migrants : Legal and Illegal

Out of this rough estimate total foreign migrants estimated for each period, those who have reported their place of birth outside India stood at 314183 (39.49 per cent), 330015 (41.24 per cent) and 40803 (6.5 per cent) for the decades 1951-61, 1961-71 and 1971-91 respectively. Even if we assume that these foreign migrants reporting their place of birth correctly were legal foreign migrants in Assam in the respective periods, then the total number of illegal foreign migrants entering into

Assam during 1951-61, 1961-71 and 1971-91 would be 493027, 165446 and 645293 respectively (Table 6.19).

Table 6.19 : Composition of Foreign Migrants : Legal and Illegal

Decade/Period	*Total foreign migrants (estimated)*	*Legal foreign migrants (reporting migrants place of birth)**	*Illegal foreign*
1951-61	807210	314183	493027
1961-71	495461	330015	165446
1971-91	686344	40803	645541
Total	1989015	685001	1304014

*0-9 years' and 0-10 years' duration of international migrant for the decades 1951-61 and 1961-71 respectively and 0-19 years' duration of international migrant for the period 1971-91.

Note : Legal foreign migrants for the period 1961-71 belong to 0-10 year duration of stay, as no 0-9 year duration of stay figures are available. As mentioned in the foot note of Table 6.18, this has deflated the volume of illegal foreign migrants of the decade 1961-71 at least by 330015/10 = 33001. Thus the number of illegal foreign migrants during the decade would be 165446 + 33001 = 198447. Hence, the total number of illegal foreign migrants during the decade 1951-91 would be 1304014 + 33001 = 1337015.

Migrants and their Offspring

It is evident from Table 6.17 that Assam's population during the period covered by the study (from 1951 to 1991) had increased by 28.46 lakh through the process of migration. But in order to ascertain the total effect of the migrants on the growth of Assam's population during the period, one has to take into account the offspring of the migrants (who are by birth citizens of India till 1986). This exercise is done by applying Assam's natural growth rate to the migrant population (Tables 6.20 and 6.21). Column 2 of Table 6.21 shows that Assam's population increases by 49,15,058 during the period when both migrants and their offspring are taken into account.

Table 6.20 : Decade-wise Migrants and Vital Rates : Assam : 1951-1991

Decade (1)	*Migrant (2)*	*Birth rate (3)*	*Death rate (4)*	*Natural growth rate (5)*
1951 – 61	1067846	45.4	26.9	20.5
1961 – 71	801880	44.1	19.6	24.5
1971 – 81	488485	33.05	14.89	18.6
1981 – 91	488484	33.15	13.47	19.68

Note : (1) Column 2 figures are derived from Table 6.17
(2) Migrants in the decades 1971-81 and 1981-91 are obtained by dividing the 1971-91 migrants by 2.
(3) Column 3, 4 and 5 are taken from Table 6.8.

Table 6.21 : Migrants and their Offspring : Assam : 1951-1991

Decade	*Migrants and their off spring (cumulative)*	*Births*	*Deaths*	*No. of migrants*
(1)	*(2)*	*(3)*	*(4)*	*(5)*
1951 – 61	1067846	484802	287251	197551
1961 – 71	2067277	911669	405186	506483
1971 – 81	3062245	1012072	455968	556104
1981 – 91	4106833	1361415	553190	808225
Total	*4915058	3769958	1701595	2068363

Note : Figures in column 2 from 1961-71 decade onwards include (i) the offspring of migrants of the preceding decade (ii) migrants of the preceding decade and (iii) migrants of the decade concerned.

* Total of column 2 includes number of migrants of column 5 of the decade 1981-91 and the migrants and their offspring (cumulative) of column 2 of the same decade.

Limitations :

The accuracy of the estimates of migration made in this work is dependent on the following :

(1) Census count : Our estimates of migration are based on the assumption that the census figures are flawless i.e., these do not suffer from either under enumeration or over enumeration (enumerating the same at more than one place).

(2) Vital rates : Even if it is assumed that the census population figures are accurate, the estimates of migration are bound to be vitiated if the vital rates, viz., birth and age specific death rates are not reflective of the ground realities. As mentioned earlier the SRS has been providing annual estimates of birth and death rates since 1968 (for the earlier periods these rates were taken the census reports). Although the SRS estimates of vital rates are believed to be more - or - less reliable, the wide year-to-year fluctuations in these rates raise doubts about their hundred per cent authenticity (an attempt has been made to remove some of these fluctuations, especially in birth rates, by using the technique of moving average). In addition to the year-to-year fluctuations in crude birth and death rates, considerable age-to-age fluctuations are noticed in the case of age specific mortality rates, which are also smoothened by using the least square method. Even after smoothening the fluctuations, we cannot claim cent per cent authenticity of the rates in reflecting the ground reality. To the extent to which the vital rates are divergent from the actual rates, our estimates of migration are erroneous.

(3) Smoothening of age group population : We have smoothened census age group population so as to yield age ratios close to 100 by using appropriate demographic techniques, as reporting of age in Indian censuses is defective. However, over a longer period of time, encompassing a number of decades, there may be major upheavals in population changes owing to a large number of factors, including migration. In such cases the age ratio may substantially deviate from 100 even if age reporting is good.[3]

References

1. H.S. Shryock, *Methods and Materials of Demography*, *op cit.*, p. 376
2. *ibid*, pp. 361-362
3. *ibid*, pp. 124-125

Index